Crochet for Absolute Beginners

From Your First Stitch to Your First Masterpiece

Discover the Art of Crochet with Ease and Creativity

Livia Fontane

From Your First Stitch to Your First Masterpiece 1
Discover the Art of Crochet with Ease and Creativity 1
Livia Fontane 1
1. Welcome to the World of Crochet! 7
    1.1 The Magic of Crochet 10
    1.2 Basic Tools and Materials 13
    1.3 What to Expect from This Book 16
2. Before You Begin: Getting to Know Your Crochet Kit 18
    2.1 Guide to Yarn Types 20
    2.2 Choosing your first crochet project 23
3. The Basics of Crochet 25
    3.1 The Slip Knot: The First Step 31
    3.2 The foundation chain: creating a base 33
    3.3 The First Stitches: Single Crochet and Double Crochet 35
    3.4 V Stitch, Granny Stitch, Fan Stitch 37
4. Reading crochet diagrams and instructions 40
    4.1 Understanding Crochet Symbols 44
    4.2 Reading written instructions 46
    4.3 Practical examples of diagrams 49
5. Basic Crochet Techniques 52
    5.1 Increases and decreases 54
    5.2 Changing color 56
    5.3 Finishing a crochet project 58
6. Projects for beginners 60
    6.1 Creating a crochet potholder 64
    6.2 Making a centerpiece 67
    6.3 Creation of Coasters and Placemats 75
7. Solving common mistakes 78
    7.1 Identifying basic crochet mistakes 80
    7.2 Correcting mistakes without having to start over 82
    7.3 Preventing common mistakes 84
8. Beyond the Basics: Next Steps in Crochet 86
    8.1 Tunisian Crochet 88
    8.2 Working in the round 91
    8.3 Combining colors and texture 94

9. Conclusion: Your creative journey continues 97
    9.1 Finding inspiration for new crochet projects 99
    9.2 Resources and online communities 101

© **Copyright 2025 by Livia Fontane – all rights reserved.** This document is intended to provide accurate and reliable information regarding the topic and issues discussed. It is sold with the understanding that the publisher is not obligated to provide accounting, officially authorized, or otherwise qualified services. If legal or professional advice is required, a qualified professional should be consulted. No part of this document may be reproduced, duplicated, or transmitted in any form, whether electronic or printed. Recording this publication is strictly prohibited, and storing this document is not permitted without written authorization from the publisher. All rights reserved.

1. Welcome to the World of Crochet!

Welcome to the Wonderful World of Crochet!

Crochet is an ancient art that has traveled through centuries to reach us, carrying a rich tradition of creativity and craftsmanship that continues to captivate generations of enthusiasts. More than just a hobby, crochet is a form of self-expression, a relaxing escape, and a way to create unique, personalized pieces.

Whether you're looking for a new pastime or hoping to rekindle a forgotten passion, this book is the perfect guide to help you embark on your journey into the fascinating world of crochet. In this introductory chapter, we'll explore the essentials—from the fundamental tools to the materials you'll need—to set you up for success.

To get started, it's essential to become familiar with the basic tools that will accompany you in every crochet project. The first and most important tool is, of course, the crochet hook. Hooks come in a variety of materials, including metal, plastic, and wood, and in different sizes—ranging from very small ones for intricate details and fine yarns to larger ones ideal for thick yarns and voluminous projects. Choosing the right hook depends on the type of yarn you plan to use and the project you have in mind.

Another essential tool is the yarn itself. Yarns are made from various materials, such as cotton, wool, acrylic, and fiber blends. Each type has unique characteristics, including softness, durability, and ease of use, all of which will impact the final result of your work. Selecting the right yarn for your project is crucial, so be sure to follow the specific recommendations provided in the instructions.

In addition to the crochet hook and yarn, several other useful tools can help you work with greater precision and ease. Stitch markers are especially handy for keeping track of stitches and rows, preventing mistakes, and simplifying counting.

Sharp-tipped scissors are essential for making clean, precise cuts on your yarn. A yarn needle, with an eye large enough to thread yarn through, is useful for weaving in loose ends and sewing different parts of your project together. Finally, a measuring tape will help ensure your work meets the correct dimensions as specified in the instructions.

These simple yet essential tools will make your crochet experience smoother and more enjoyable, allowing you to focus on the creative process.

Now that we have an overview of the essential tools, let's move on to materials. As mentioned earlier, yarns come in a wide variety of materials and thicknesses.

Cotton is a popular choice for beginners due to its durability and ease of use. It's ideal for projects like doilies, potholders, and lightweight garments. Wool, on the other hand, is perfect for creating warm and cozy pieces such as scarves, hats, and blankets. Acrylic is an affordable and versatile option, available in a vast range of colors and suitable for many different projects.

Fiber blends combine the best qualities of various materials, offering softness, durability, and easy maintenance. Choosing the right yarn for your project will enhance both the process and the final result, ensuring a smooth and enjoyable crochet experience.

Another important aspect to consider is yarn tension, which refers to the amount of pressure applied to the yarn as you work. Tension directly affects the size and texture of your project.

If the tension is too tight, the fabric will be stiff and difficult to handle; if it's too loose, the work may become too soft and lose its shape. Finding the right balance is essential for achieving a polished and professional-looking result. This takes practice and experimentation, so don't be afraid to adjust and refine your technique as you go.

Now that we've explored the essential tools and materials, let's take a look at what you can expect from this book. *Crochet for Beginners* is designed to guide you step by step through your learning journey. Each chapter focuses on a specific aspect of crochet, starting with the fundamentals and progressing to more advanced techniques.

We'll begin with the very first steps, such as the slip knot and foundation chain, before moving on to essential stitches like single crochet and double crochet. You'll learn how to read patterns and diagrams, make increases and decreases, and seamlessly change colors.

Every technique is explained in detail, with illustrations and photographs to guide you through each step, ensuring a smooth and enjoyable learning experience

.

But we won't stop there! Once you've mastered the basics, you'll find a collection of simple yet rewarding projects designed specifically for beginners.

You'll be able to put your new skills into practice right away by creating useful and decorative items such as potholders, table centerpieces, coasters, and placemats. Each project comes with clear, step-by-step instructions to help you work with confidence and precision, ensuring a satisfying and enjoyable crochet experience.

Finally, we'll also address common mistakes that can occur while crocheting. You'll learn how to identify and fix errors without having to start over, and how to prevent the most frequent mistakes with a few simple tips. This will allow you to work with greater ease and rapidly improve your skills.

Whether you want to create a special gift for a loved one, decorate your home with unique items, or simply relax with a rewarding activity, this book will equip you with all the skills you need to turn yarn into art. Don't wait any longer—pick up your crochet hook and start creating today!

1.1 The Magic of Crochet

The art of crochet is an ancient craft that has spanned centuries and cultures, transforming simple threads into beautiful, personalized creations. The magic of crochet lies in its ability to blend tradition and innovation, allowing anyone to express their creativity through a simple tool: the crochet hook.

Although it may seem complex at first glance, crochet is actually accessible to everyone, regardless of age or experience. The history of crochet is fascinating and full of evolution. Its origins are uncertain, but it's believed to have ancient roots, with examples of crochet-like work found across various cultures, from Egyptian artifacts to Chinese creations.

Over the centuries, crochet has traveled across continents, adapting and transforming according to local traditions. For instance, during the 19th-century potato famine in Ireland, crochet became a source of livelihood for many families, who sold their intricate works to earn money. This period saw the birth of the famous Irish lace, one of the most refined and admired crochet techniques in the world.

Crochet is not just a manual technique; it is also a means of artistic expression. With just a crochet hook and some yarn, you can create a wide range of items—from clothing and home accessories to Christmas decorations and amigurumi, the small Japanese stuffed toys. Each creation is unique and reflects the personality and creativity of the maker.

For example, a crocheted scarf can be simple and functional, or elaborate and adorned with intricate patterns, depending on the creator's preferences. The versatility of crochet allows you to experiment with colors, textures, and shapes, bringing to life one-of-a-kind works of art that are truly irreplaceable.

One of the most fascinating aspects of crochet is its ability to create connections. While crochet can be a solitary activity, it's also a way to connect with others who share the same passion. There are numerous online communities and local crochet groups where you can exchange ideas, advice, and projects. These groups offer invaluable support, especially for beginners, who can find inspiration and encouragement.

Additionally, joining these communities allows you to discover new techniques and trends, keeping your passion for crochet alive and thriving.

The magic of crochet also lies in its ability to relax and reduce stress. Numerous studies have shown that hands-on activities, like crochet, can have beneficial effects on mental health by reducing anxiety and improving mood. The repetitive motion of crocheting has a meditative effect, helping to calm the mind and focus on the present moment.

Many people find crochet to be a way to disconnect from the hectic pace of daily life and engage in an activity that requires patience and attention. This process of slow, deliberate creation serves as an antidote to the fast-paced, instant-gratification culture that defines the modern world.

Another interesting aspect of crochet is its sustainability. In an era where environmental awareness is becoming increasingly important, crochet offers an eco-friendly alternative to mass production. By using natural and recycled yarns, it's possible to create durable, high-quality items while reducing environmental impact.

Additionally, crochet allows you to breathe new life into old clothing or fabrics, transforming them into new creations. For example, an old sweater can be unraveled, and the yarn reused to make a blanket or cushion. This sustainable approach not only reduces waste but also encourages more mindful and responsible consumption.

The magic of crochet also lies in its ability to adapt to the needs and tastes of those who practice it. Whether you're a beginner or an expert, crochet offers endless possibilities for experimentation and learning. Every new project is an opportunity to improve your skills and discover new techniques.

For example, after mastering the basic stitches, you can explore more advanced techniques such as Tunisian crochet or working in the round. Each technique adds a new level of complexity and interest, keeping your passion for crochet alive and ever-evolving.

Moreover, crochet is an art that can be passed down through generations. Many people have learned to crochet from their parents or grandparents, creating a special bond with their family and their history. Teaching crochet to your children or grandchildren is a way to share a passion and pass on important values such as patience, creativity, and attention to detail.

This transfer of knowledge and skills creates a sense of continuity and belonging, strengthening both family and cultural ties.

Finally, the magic of crochet lies in its ability to surprise and enchant. Every new project is both a challenge and a discovery, a creative journey that leads to unexpected and rewarding results. Whether it's a simple cowl or an intricate bedspread, every creation is a unique masterpiece, the product of effort, dedication, and a deep love for the art of crochet.

This ability to transform a simple thread into something beautiful and meaningful is what makes crochet such a special and captivating art. With each stitch, each round, and each completed project, crochet reminds us that true magic lies in our ability to create and transform the world around us.

1.2 Basic Tools and Materials

To begin your journey into the world of crochet, it's essential to understand the basic tools and materials that will accompany you throughout each project. Although crochet may seem simple, it requires a specific set of tools that, when chosen and used correctly, can make the difference between a well-crafted piece and one that could lead to frustration.

The first essential tool is, of course, the crochet hook itself. Crochet hooks are available in a variety of materials, including metal, plastic, wood, and bamboo. Each material has its unique characteristics: metal hooks, for example, are sturdy and durable, ideal for projects that require precision and consistent tension, while bamboo or wooden hooks offer a warmer, more natural grip, perfect for those who prefer an organic feel while working.

The choice of crochet hook material can significantly affect your crochet experience, so it's a good idea to try different types to find the one that best suits your style.

Another crucial aspect is the size of the crochet hook, which ranges from very small to very large. The sizes are typically indicated in millimeters or with a numbering system specific to each country. A smaller hook is ideal for detailed work and fine yarns, while a larger one is perfect for bulky projects and thick yarns.

It's important to note that the size of the hook should be chosen based on the type of yarn you're using, as an incorrect pairing can affect the quality of the finished piece. For instance, a hook that's too large for a thin yarn could result in loose and poorly defined stitches, while a hook that's too small for thick yarn could make the work stiff and difficult to handle.

When it comes to yarn, the variety available on the market is vast and can be a bit overwhelming for beginners. Yarn differs in thickness, material, and texture. The most common types are made from wool, cotton, acrylic, and blends.

Wool is valued for its elasticity and warmth, making it ideal for winter garments like scarves and hats. Cotton, on the other hand, is less elastic but very durable and breathable, perfect for summer projects like tops and bags. Acrylic is an affordable and versatile option, easy to wash, and comes in a wide range of colors. Blended yarns combine the properties of different materials, offering a balance between strength, softness, and ease of maintenance.

When choosing a yarn, consider not only the aesthetic appeal but also the practicality and intended use of the project. For example, for a project intended for a baby, it's better to choose a hypoallergenic and soft yarn, such as organic cotton.

In addition to crochet hooks and yarn, there are other essential accessories that will make your work easier and more enjoyable. Stitch markers, for example, are small tools that help you keep track of stitches or sections of your project, especially useful for complex or large-scale projects.

Sewing scissors are another fundamental accessory, necessary for cutting the yarn precisely without fraying it. A yarn needle, with a large enough eye to accommodate the yarn, is indispensable for hiding yarn ends in the finished work, ensuring a clean and professional appearance. A measuring tape is also useful for measuring the dimensions of your project, ensuring that they match the desired specifications.

.

Another tool that can be incredibly helpful, especially for beginners, is a reference book or guide. While many resources are available online today, having a physical book with detailed explanations, illustrations, and diagrams can be a great asset. A good crochet book for beginners should not only cover the basic techniques but also provide practical tips on how to avoid and correct common mistakes. Additionally, many books include simple projects that allow you to immediately put what you've learned into practice, offering a sense of accomplishment and motivation.

Finally, don't underestimate the importance of a good working environment. Make sure you have a well-lit and comfortable space where you can work without distractions. An ergonomic chair and a table at the right height can make a big difference, especially if you plan to work for extended periods. Organize your tools and materials neatly, perhaps using boxes or containers specifically designed for crochet hooks and yarn, so everything is within reach and your workspace stays clean and tidy.

Knowing and properly using the basic tools and materials is the first step in becoming a skilled crocheter. Every project, big or small, begins with the right choice of tools and understanding their characteristics. Take the time to explore the different options available and experiment with various materials and techniques. Remember that crochet is an art that requires patience and practice, but with the right tools and a little dedication, you'll be able to create unique and personal masterpieces. Happy crafting and enjoy your journey into the wonderful world of crochet!

1.3 What to Expect from This Book

Starting a journey in the art of crochet may seem like a daunting task, but with *Crochet for Beginners* by your side, you'll discover that it's a fascinating and rewarding adventure. This book has been carefully designed to guide you step by step, from the fundamental basics to the creation of more complex projects, with the goal of making the learning process as simple and enjoyable as possible.

The book is structured in a way that will guide you through every stage of your learning journey. We will start with an overview of the basic tools and materials needed to begin crocheting. You will learn about the different types of hooks, yarns, and essential accessories. This section is crucial because a good understanding of the basic tools will allow you to work with more confidence and precision. For example, you will discover that there are crochet hooks of various sizes and materials, each suited for specific types of yarn and projects.

Once you've familiarized yourself with the tools, we will move on to the basic crochet techniques. The book will guide you through the first steps, such as the slip knot and the foundation chain, which form the basis of any crochet project. Each technique is explained in detail, with step-by-step illustrations showing you exactly how to perform each movement. This visual approach is especially helpful for beginners, as it allows you to clearly see how each step should look. Additionally, you will find practical tips to avoid common mistakes, such as irregular yarn tension or choosing the wrong yarn for a specific project.

As you gain confidence with the basic techniques, the book will introduce you to more complex stitches, such as the single crochet and double crochet, as well as more elaborate patterns like the V Stitch, Granny Square, and Fan Stitch. Each new stitch is accompanied by detailed explanations and illustrations, helping you understand not only how to execute the stitch but also how to use it in various projects. For example, the Granny Square is often used to create blankets and scarves, while the Fan Stitch can add a decorative touch to a cushion cover or a bag.

In addition to teaching you the techniques, *Crochet for Beginners* inspires you to unleash your creativity with a series of simple and rewarding projects. Whether you want to create a potholder, a table centerpiece, or a coaster, you'll find detailed instructions and helpful tips for each project. Every section of the book is designed to gradually build your skills, allowing you to immediately apply what you've learned. For example, once you've mastered the basic stitches, you might want to try making a potholder. The book will guide you through every stage of the project, from choosing the right yarn and crochet hook to reading the patterns and instructions, all the way to finishing your work.

Another important aspect of the book is its focus on preventing and correcting common mistakes. You will learn how to identify and fix errors without having to start over, saving you time and frustration. For example, if you realize you've skipped a stitch in a previous row, the book will show you how to go back and correct the mistake without compromising the entire project. Additionally, you will find tips on how to maintain consistent tension in your yarn, how to avoid your work from curling or distorting, and how to choose the colors and textures that best suit your project.

Once you have gained a solid understanding of the basics of crochet, the book will introduce you to advanced techniques and more complex projects. You will discover Tunisian crochet, working in the round, and how to combine colors and textures to create unique, personalized works of art. Additionally, the book will provide resources and tips on how to find inspiration for new projects, both online and within your local community.

With clear explanations, detailed illustrations, and practical tips, this book will provide you with all the skills necessary to turn yarn into art. Whether you're a complete beginner or already have some experience with crochet, you'll find everything you need in these pages to improve your skills and create unique masterpieces. So, grab your crochet hook and start exploring the wonderful world of crochet with confidence and creativity.

2. Before You Begin: Getting to Know Your Crochet Kit

Before you begin your journey into the fascinating world of crochet, it is essential to get to know your crochet kit. This chapter will guide you through the essential tools, various types of hooks and yarns, and how to choose the right materials for your projects. Let's start with the basic tools.

The first and most important tool is, of course, the crochet hook. Crochet hooks come in a variety of materials, including metal, plastic, wood, and bamboo. Each material has its unique characteristics: metal hooks are sturdy and durable, ideal for projects that require precision; plastic hooks are lightweight and often more affordable, making them perfect for beginners; while wooden and bamboo hooks provide a warm, natural feel and are particularly appreciated for their lightness and comfort during extended use. The choice of material depends on your personal preferences and the type of project you plan to create.

In addition to the material, crochet hooks also vary in terms of size. The size of the hook is determined by the diameter of its shaft, which can range from very small (for detailed work and fine yarns) to very large (for thick yarns and bulky projects). Sizes are typically indicated in millimeters or by a specific numbering system, depending on the brand and country of production.

It is important to choose the hook size based on the type of yarn you will use and the final result you wish to achieve. For example, a larger hook will create wider stitches and a softer fabric, while a smaller hook will produce tighter stitches and a denser fabric.

Now, let's talk about yarns. Yarns come in a wide variety of materials, colors, and thicknesses. The most common materials include wool, cotton, acrylic, and blends. Wool is warm and elastic, making it ideal for winter garments like scarves, hats, and sweaters. Cotton is cool and breathable, perfect for summer projects like tops, bags, and home decor items. Acrylic is affordable and versatile, suitable for a wide range of projects, from toys to clothing items. Blended yarns combine the properties of different materials to offer specific benefits, such as the softness of wool and the durability of cotton.

The choice of yarn depends on the project you have in mind and your personal preferences. It's also important to consider the yarn weight, which can range from very thin (lace) to very thick (super bulky). The yarn weight will influence the final result of your work and the size of the crochet hook you need to use. Every yarn comes with a label that indicates its weight, composition, care instructions, and the recommended crochet hook size. Carefully reading these details will help you make the right choice for your project.

In addition to crochet hooks and yarns, there are other tools that can make your crochet work easier. For example, stitch markers are small tools that help you mark specific stitches in your work, such as the beginning of a round or an increase or decrease stitch. Row counters are useful for tracking the rows or rounds you've completed, especially for complex projects. Scissors are essential for cutting yarn neatly and precisely. Yarn needles, with their rounded tip and large eye, are used to hide yarn ends and sew together parts of your project.

Now that you have an overview of the essential tools, it's time to choose your first project. For beginners, it's advisable to start with a simple project that allows you to become familiar with basic stitches and fundamental techniques. An ideal project might be a placemat, a pot holder, or a coaster. These projects don't take much time and will give you the satisfaction of quickly seeing the results of your work. When choosing your first project, also consider the type of yarn and the recommended crochet hook size. Following the pattern instructions will help you achieve a satisfying result and avoid frustration.

Choosing the right tools and materials will allow you to work with ease and achieve better results. Remember that practice is key: the more time you dedicate to crochet, the more you'll improve your skills and discover new techniques. Don't be afraid to experiment with different materials and projects: crochet is a versatile and creative art that offers endless possibilities. Happy crocheting and have fun!

2.1 Guide to Yarn Types

When you begin exploring the world of crochet, one of the first things you'll discover is the vast array of yarns available. Choosing the right yarn is crucial to the success of your project, as it affects not only the final appearance of your work but also how easy it is to work with and the durability of the finished product. There are many types of yarns, each with its own unique characteristics, that can be used to create a variety of items, from clothing to home accessories. In this guide, we will explore the different types of yarns, how to recognize the ideal quality and consistency for various projects, and provide tips on how to choose the right yarn based on the desired outcome.

First and foremost, it is important to understand the different materials that yarns can be made from. Natural fibers such as cotton, wool, linen, and silk are highly valued for their quality and unique properties. Cotton, for example, is a very versatile yarn, ideal for summer projects like tops, bags, and home accessories. It is durable, easy to work with, and available in a wide range of colors. Wool, on the other hand, is perfect for winter projects like scarves, hats, and sweaters due to its ability to retain warmth. There are different types of wool, such as merino, which is particularly soft and comfortable, and lamb's wool, which is stronger and more durable. Linen is another highly regarded natural fiber, known for its strength and ability to absorb moisture, making it ideal for summer garments and home accessories. Finally, silk is a luxurious and shiny yarn, perfect for elegant and sophisticated projects.

In addition to natural yarns, there are also synthetic yarns, such as acrylic, nylon, and polyester. These yarns are often more affordable than natural ones and offer a wide range of colors and textures. Acrylic, for example, is a very popular yarn for beginners because it is easy to work with, durable, and machine washable. However, it is important to note that synthetic yarns can be less breathable than natural fibers and may not be as comfortable to wear. Nylon and polyester are often used in combination with other yarns to add strength and durability to projects.

Another important factor to consider when choosing yarn is its weight. Yarn weight refers to the thickness of the yarn and can range from very thin (lace) to very thick (super bulky). The weight of the yarn affects the size of the finished project and the size of the crochet hook to use. For example, a very thin yarn will require a smaller hook and will produce a more delicate and detailed fabric, while a very thick yarn will require a larger hook and will create a thicker, more robust fabric. It's important to choose the yarn weight based on the type of project you want to create and the pattern instructions you are following.

The texture of the yarn is another crucial factor to consider. Some yarns are smooth and uniform, while others may have a rougher or more irregular texture. The texture of the yarn can affect the final appearance of the project and the ease of working with it. For example, a smooth and uniform yarn is ideal for projects that require detailed and precise stitches, such as lacework or intricate patterns. A yarn with a rougher or more irregular texture can add visual and tactile interest to simpler projects, like scarves or blankets.

When choosing a yarn, it's also important to consider the color. The color of the yarn can influence the final appearance of the project and how the stitches and patterns are visible. Solid color yarns are ideal for projects that require detailed stitches and intricate patterns, as they allow each stitch to be clearly seen. Variegated yarns, which change color along the thread, can add visual interest to simpler projects and create unique and surprising effects. It's important to choose a color that suits the project you want to create and that you enjoy working with.

Finally, it's important to consider the quality of the yarn. A high-quality yarn will be easier to work with, produce a more uniform fabric, and last longer. When purchasing yarn, it's helpful to read reviews and ask for recommendations from other crochet enthusiasts. Additionally, you can make a small test swatch to see how the yarn behaves and how the finished fabric looks. This can help avoid disappointments and ensure that the final project turns out exactly as you envisioned.

Choosing the right yarn is a crucial step for the success of your crochet project. Understanding the different types of yarn, knowing their characteristics, and selecting the right yarn based on the desired outcome can make the difference between a mediocre project and a masterpiece. Take the time to explore the different options available, do some testing, and ask for advice. With a bit of practice and experience, you'll be able to choose the perfect yarn for every project and turn thread into art.

2.2 Choosing your first crochet project

Choosing your first crochet project is a crucial step in your creative journey and can greatly impact the success and satisfaction you'll get from this new adventure. As a beginner, it's important to select a project that is manageable and allows you to gain confidence in your skills without feeling overwhelmed. The key to a rewarding first experience is finding a balance between the complexity of the design and the time it takes to complete it. Starting with something too complicated might lead to frustration, while a project that's too simple may not give you the sense of accomplishment you're looking for.

A great starting point is to choose a project that uses the basic stitches you've just learned, like the single crochet and double crochet. These stitches are fundamental and form the base for many more complex designs. A perfect example of an initial project could be a simple scarf or a pot holder. Scarves are ideal because they only require the repetition of basic stitches along the entire length of the project, allowing you to practice and refine your technique without dealing with changes in direction or complicated patterns. Plus, a scarf is a useful and rewarding accessory to wear or gift.

Another great project for beginners is a pot holder. Pot holders are small, so they can be completed in a relatively short time, giving you a quick sense of accomplishment. Additionally, since pot holders are often made with thicker yarns, they are easy to handle, and the stitches are more visible, making learning easier. You can start with a simple square pot holder using only single crochet, and as you gain confidence, you can experiment with striped patterns or color changes.

If you prefer something decorative, a table centerpiece might be the right project for you. Again, you can start with a simple design using only the basic stitches. A round or square centerpiece can be made with a series of chains and single crochet stitches, and it can be a stylish addition to your home or a handmade gift for a friend or family member.

When choosing your first project, it's also important to consider the type of yarn and color. Thicker yarns are generally easier to work with for beginners because the stitches are larger and more visible. Additionally, light colors can help you see the stitches more clearly, while dark colors may be harder to work with, especially when you're still learning to identify the different stitches.

Another factor to consider is the amount of time you have available for crocheting. If you only have short moments throughout the day, a smaller project like a potholder or a coaster might be more suitable. On the other hand, if you have more time to dedicate and want a project that will keep you engaged for a while, a scarf or a table centerpiece could be more rewarding.

To help you choose the right project, you might also consider joining an online community of crochet enthusiasts. There are many groups on platforms like Facebook, Reddit, and Instagram where you can find inspiration, ask for advice, and share your progress. These communities can be a valuable source of support and motivation, especially when you encounter difficulties or need encouragement.

Additionally, many websites and crochet blogs offer free patterns and step-by-step tutorials that can guide you through your first project. These patterns often include detailed photographs and video tutorials that can help you visualize each step and better understand how to execute the stitches.

Another helpful tip is to keep a crochet journal. You can note down the projects you've completed, the stitches you've learned, and the challenges you've faced. This journal will not only help you track your progress but will also be a source of inspiration when you look back and see how much you've improved.

Finally, remember that crochet is an art that requires patience and practice. Don't get discouraged if your first project isn't perfect. Every stitch you make brings you one step closer to becoming a crochet expert. With time and practice, you'll be able to tackle more complex projects and create unique, personal masterpieces. Enjoy your work and have fun with your first crochet project!

3. The Basics of Crochet

Crochet is an ancient and fascinating art that has spanned centuries and cultures, carrying with it the ability to transform simple threads into intricate and useful works of art. To begin your journey into the world of crochet, it is essential to learn the basics, which form the foundation for any future project. In this chapter, we will focus on three essential elements: the slip knot, the foundation chain, and the first basic stitches, such as the single crochet and double crochet. These elements are the building blocks upon which you will create all your future crochet projects.

The first step to start crocheting is learning how to make a slip knot. This knot is the starting point for any crochet project and serves to securely attach the yarn to the hook. To make a slip knot, take the yarn and create a loop, then pass the end of the yarn through the loop and gently pull to tighten. Insert the hook into the loop and pull the yarn until the knot tightens around the hook, but not too tightly to prevent movement. This knot will allow you to begin your foundation chain, which is the next fundamental step.

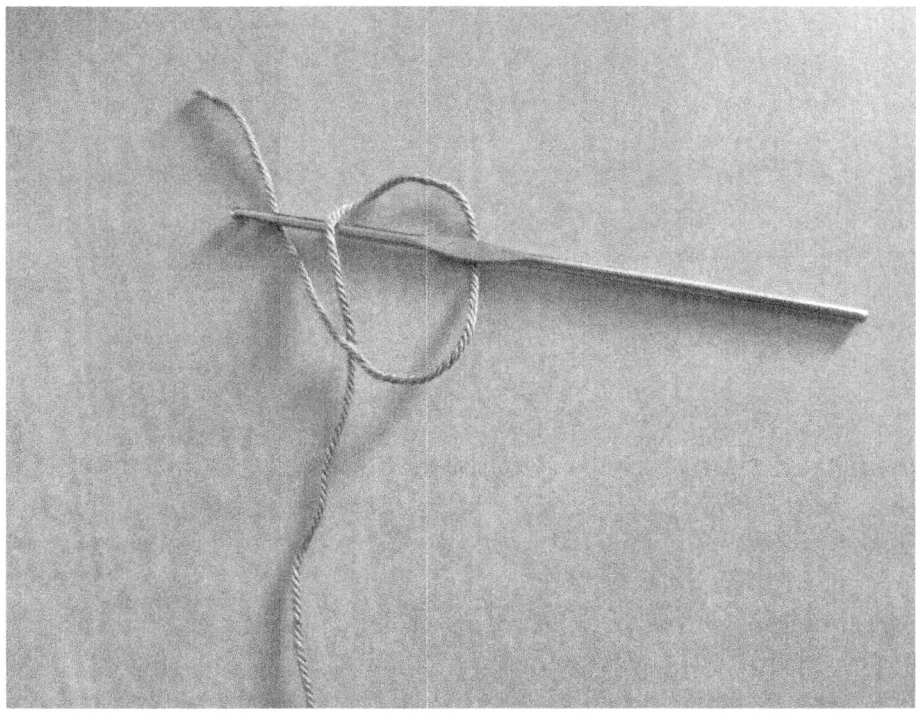

a) Take the yarn and create a loop

b) Pass the end of the yarn through the loop and gently pull to tighten
c) Insert the crochet hook into the loop and pull the yarn until the knot tightens around the hook, but not too tight to prevent movement

a) The foundation chain is essential for creating a solid base for your crochet work. To begin, hold the crochet hook with the slip knot in your right hand (or left hand if you're left-handed) and the yarn in your opposite hand. Wrap the yarn around the hook and pull it through the slip knot to create the first chain stitch. Continue wrapping the yarn around the hook and pulling it through the loop just created, repeating this motion until you reach the desired length for your foundation chain. Each loop you create is a chain stitch, and the length of your chain will determine the width of your project.
b) Hold the crochet hook with the slip knot in your right hand (or left hand if you're left-handed) and the yarn in your opposite hand.

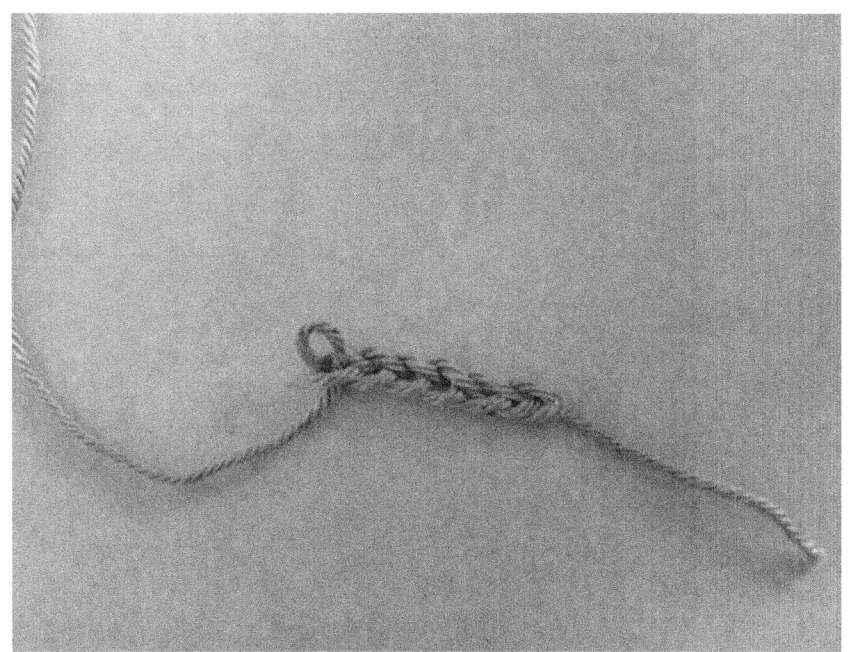

a) Hold the crochet hook with the slip knot in your right hand (or left hand if you're left-handed) and the yarn in your opposite hand

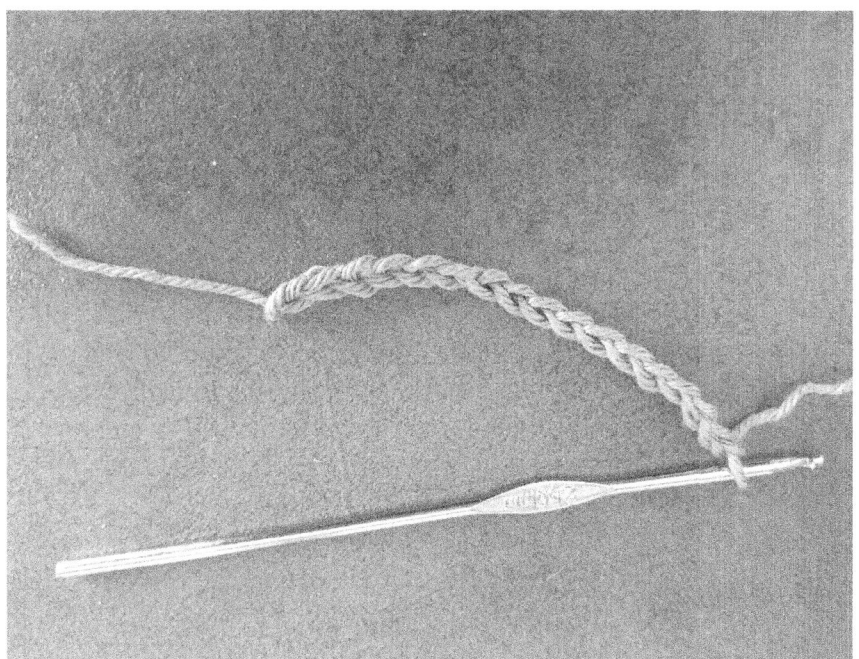

b) Wrap the yarn around the crochet hook and pull it through the slip knot to create the first chain stitch
c) Continue wrapping the yarn around the hook and pulling it through the loop you just created, repeating this motion until you reach the desired length for your foundation chain

Once you've completed your foundation chain, it's time to learn the first fundamental stitches: the single crochet and the double crochet. These stitches are the foundation of many crochet patterns and projects, and they will allow you to create a variety of textures and designs.

The single crochet is one of the simplest and most common stitches. To make a single crochet, insert the hook into the second chain from your hook, yarn over, and pull through the chain. Now you have two loops on your hook. Yarn over again and pull through both loops. You've just completed your first single crochet. Continue working single crochet stitches across the entire length of your foundation chain.

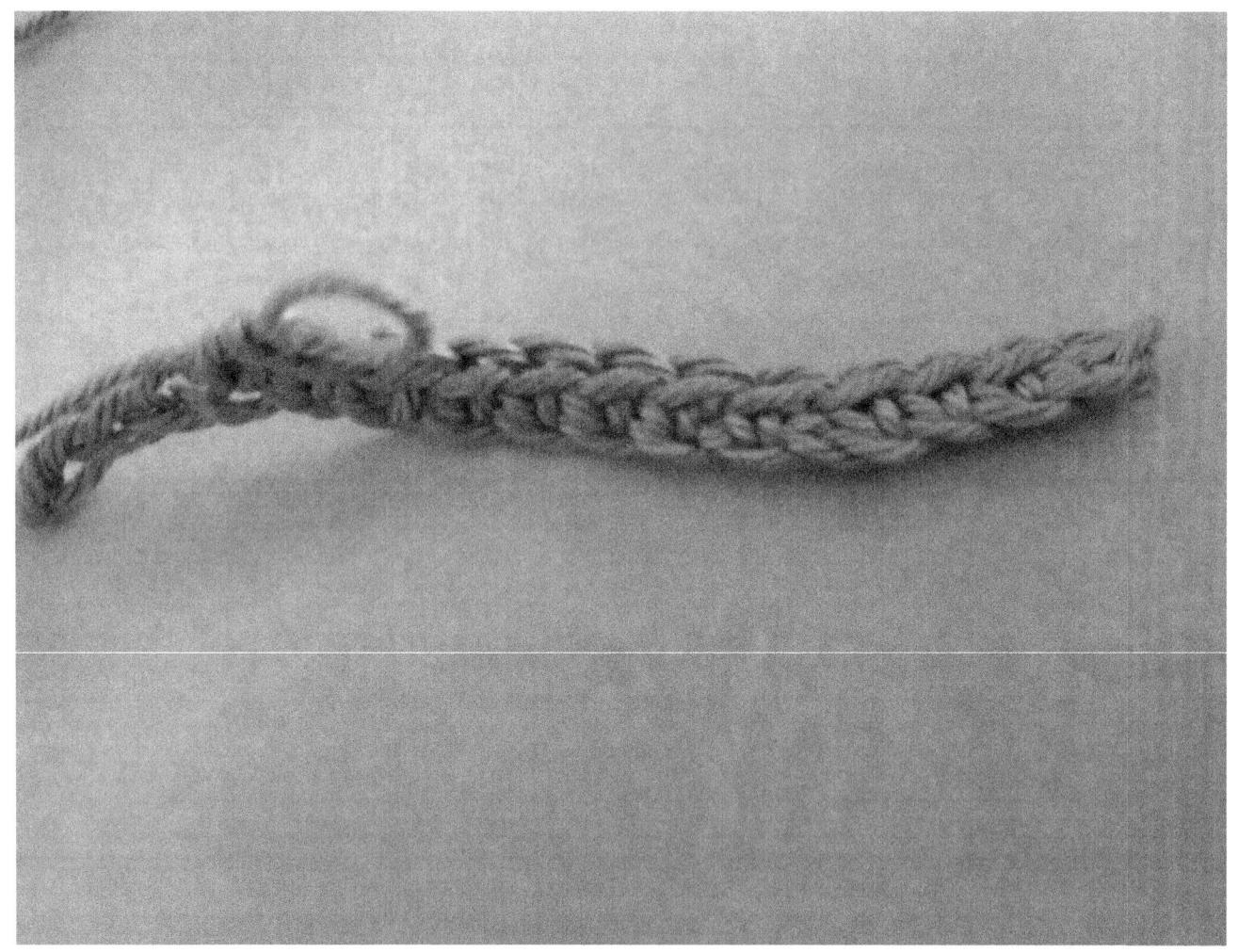

Single Crochet

The double crochet, on the other hand, is a bit more complex but just as fundamental. To make a double crochet, wrap the yarn around the hook before inserting it into the third chain from your hook. Wrap the yarn around the hook again and pull through the chain, now having three loops on the hook. Wrap the yarn around the hook and pull through the first two loops, leaving two loops on the hook. Wrap the yarn around the hook again and pull through the remaining two loops. You've just completed your first double crochet. Continue working double crochets along the entire length of your foundation chain.

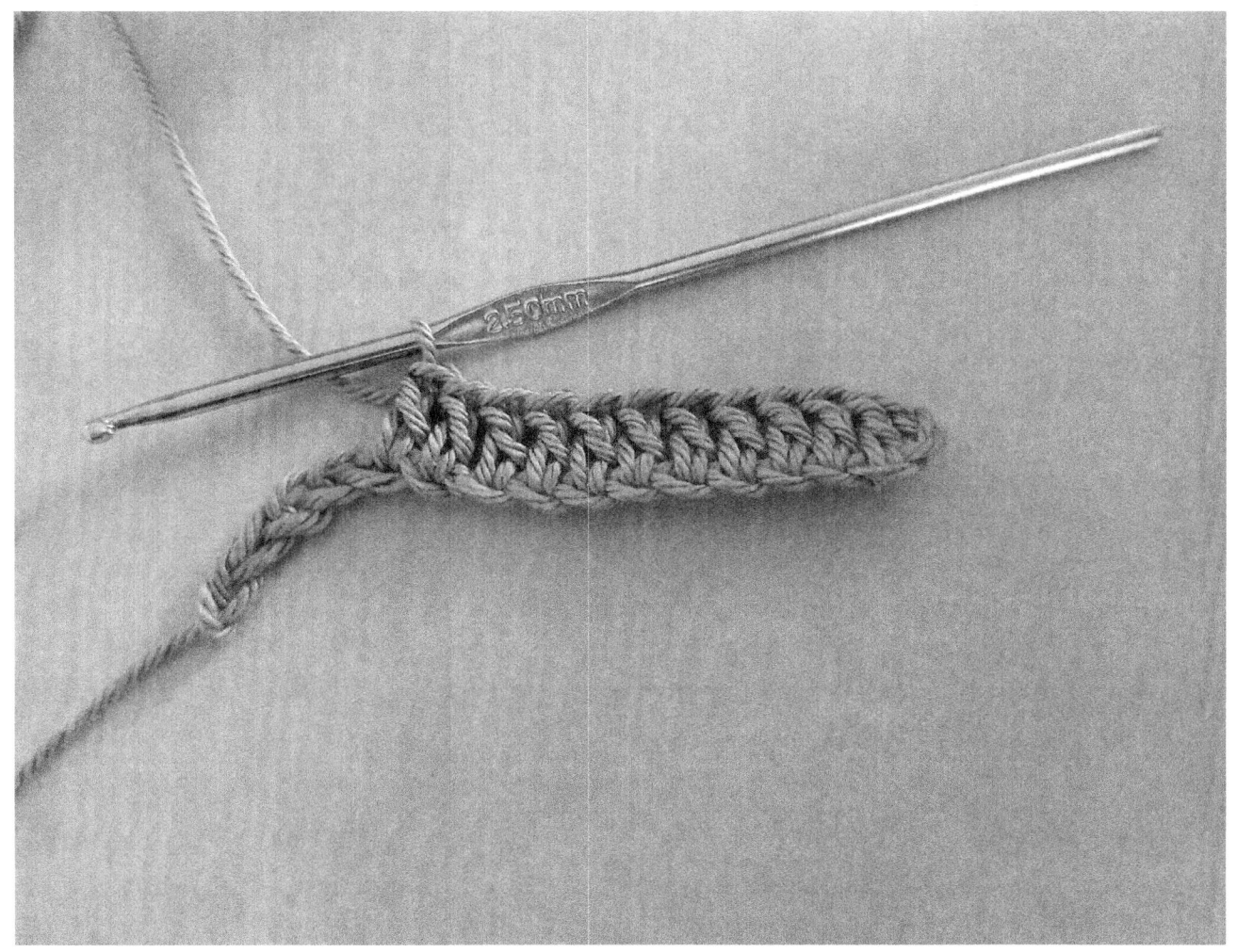

Double Crochet

These fundamental stitches, the single crochet and double crochet, can be combined in various ways to create a wide range of textures and designs. For example, by alternating single crochets and double crochets, you can create a striped pattern that adds visual interest to your project. Additionally, learning to work in the round with these stitches will allow you to create three-dimensional items like hats, bags, and amigurumi.

While practicing these stitches, it's important to maintain a consistent yarn tension to ensure your stitches are even. If your stitches are too tight, your work will be stiff and difficult to handle; if they're too loose, your work will be floppy and may not hold the desired shape. Find a balance that allows you to work comfortably and with ease.

Another crucial aspect of learning crochet is understanding the symbols and abbreviations commonly used in patterns and instructions. For example, the single crochet is often abbreviated as "sc" and the double crochet as "dc." Familiarizing yourself with these symbols will help you follow patterns more easily and understand written instructions.

As you gain confidence with the slip knot, the foundation chain, and the basic stitches, you'll start to see how these elements come together to create complete projects. You might begin with simple projects like a scarf or a square for a blanket, which will allow you to practice your new stitches in a practical context. Over time and with practice, you'll be able to tackle more complex projects and experiment with different types of yarns and colors.

Remember that crochet is an art that requires patience and practice. Don't get discouraged if your first attempts aren't perfect; every mistake is an opportunity to learn and improve. With dedication and perseverance, you'll discover that crochet can be an incredibly rewarding and relaxing activity, capable of transforming simple threads into unique masterpieces.

Mastering the basics of crochet is the first step towards creating beautiful handmade projects. The slip knot, the foundation chain, and the fundamental stitches like the single crochet and the double crochet are the essential tools that will guide you through every stage of your crochet journey. With practice and passion, you'll discover that crochet is not just a hobby, but an art that allows you to express your creativity and create unique and meaningful items. Happy crocheting!

3.1 The Slip Knot: The First Step

The slip knot is the first essential step to start any crochet project. This seemingly simple technique is the foundation upon which you will build all your future creations. Learning to make a slip knot correctly is crucial to ensure that your work is stable and well-structured from the very beginning. In this subchapter, I will guide you through every detail of this crucial step, providing you with clear and illustrated instructions to help you master this technique.

To begin, take your yarn and form a loop, leaving a tail of about 10-15 centimeters. This loop will be the base of your slip knot. Now, with the yarn on the right side of the loop, pass a part of the yarn through the loop, creating a small hitch. This hitch is where you will insert your hook. Gently pull the yarn to tighten the loop around the hook, but not too tightly, so it can slide easily along the yarn. This is your basic slip knot.

An important aspect of the slip knot is its ability to be adjusted. This means that you can tighten or loosen it depending on the needs of your project. To tighten the knot, pull the yarn that connects to the ball of yarn, while holding the loop steady with the hook. To loosen it, gently pull the yarn tail. This feature makes the slip knot particularly useful for starting projects that require flexibility in yarn tension.

A practical example of using the slip knot is the creation of a foundation chain, which will be covered in the next subchapter. The foundation chain is the basis for many crochet projects, and a well-made slip knot ensures that the chain is uniform and stable. Imagine you want to create a simple scarf: you start with a slip knot, then work a series of chains until you reach the desired length. If the slip knot is not done correctly, your chain may turn out too tight or too loose, compromising the entire project.

Another example is the creation of an amigurumi, those small crochet dolls loved by both adults and children. In this case as well, the slip knot is the starting point. After making the slip knot, you begin working in the round, adding stitches and gradually increasing to shape your doll. A stable and well-made slip knot ensures that the center of your amigurumi is solid and won't come apart over time.

To help you master this technique, I recommend practicing making and undoing the slip knot several times. Take a scrap piece of yarn and a crochet hook, and try creating the slip knot, tightening it, and loosening it.

Repeat this process until you feel comfortable with the technique. You can also watch video tutorials online or follow the illustrations in this book for a visual guide.

Another helpful tip is to experiment with different types of yarn. Each yarn has a different texture and tension, and learning to make the slip knot with various types of yarn will help you become more versatile and skilled. For example, a cotton yarn might require a different tension compared to wool or acrylic yarn. Take the time to explore these differences and understand how they affect your slip knot.

Finally, remember that practice is the key to success. Don't get discouraged if your slip knot isn't perfect at first. Every mistake is an opportunity to learn and improve. With time and practice, you'll become more skilled and confident. The slip knot is just the first step on your journey into the art of crochet, but it's a crucial step that will open the door to endless creative possibilities.

The slip knot is an essential technique that every beginner must learn to start off on the right foot in the world of crochet. By following the detailed instructions and practicing regularly, you'll be able to master this technique and use it as the foundation for all your future projects. Don't underestimate the importance of this step: a well-made slip knot is the first step toward creating crochet masterpieces. Happy crocheting and have fun!

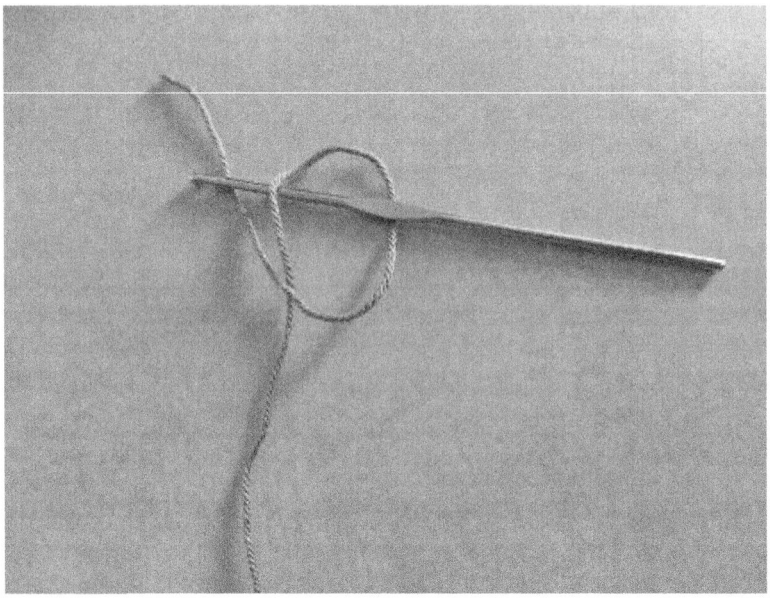

3.2 The foundation chain: creating a base

The foundation chain is the first essential step for any crochet project. It is the base on which all other stitches are built, so mastering it well is crucial. Let's begin with the choice of yarn and the appropriate crochet hook. For beginners, it is recommended to use a medium-thickness yarn and a corresponding hook size, usually indicated on the yarn label. This will make it easier to see the stitches and maintain an even tension.

To begin, hold the yarn in your left hand, wrapping it around your index finger to control the tension. With your right hand, hold the crochet hook as if it were a pen or a knife, depending on which grip feels more comfortable to you. Start with a slip knot, inserting the hook through the loop and pulling the yarn to tighten the knot onto the hook. This knot should not be too tight, as it needs to move freely along the hook.

Now, to create the foundation chain, wrap the yarn around the hook from back to front. This movement is called "yarn over." With the yarn over the hook, pull the yarn through the loop already on the hook. You've just created your first chain stitch! Continue yarn over and pull through the loop on the hook until you reach the desired number of chain stitches for your project. It's important to maintain even tension during this process to avoid the chain being too tight or too loose. A chain that's too tight will make it difficult to work the next stitches, while one that's too loose may affect the structure of the project.

A good exercise to improve your tension is to practice creating chains of different lengths. Start with short chains of 10-20 stitches and gradually increase the length. This will help you develop muscle memory and maintain consistent tension. Another useful tip is to count the chains aloud as you make them. This will help you maintain a steady rhythm and avoid losing track of the count.

Once you feel comfortable with creating the foundation chain, you can start experimenting with different tensions and yarns. For example, try using a thicker or thinner yarn and observe how your chain changes. This will give you a better understanding of how tension and yarn type affect the final result. Additionally, you can try making chains with different types of yarn, such as cotton, wool, or acrylic, to see how each behaves.

Another important aspect of the foundation chain is its versatility. It can be used as the base for a wide range of projects, from simple shawls and scarves to more complex doilies and amigurumi. For example, to create a scarf, you can start with a long foundation chain and then work low or high stitches along it. For a doily, you can start with a circular foundation chain and then work in the round. The foundation chain can also be used to create decorative edges or to add details to an existing project.

It's also helpful to know how to fix any mistakes in the foundation chain. If you notice you've made an error, such as a chain that's too tight or too loose, you can simply undo the stitches until you reach the mistake and redo them. This is one of the advantages of crochet: it's easy to correct mistakes without having to start over from the beginning.

Finally, don't forget to have fun while learning to make the foundation chain. Crochet is a creative and relaxing art, and every new stitch you learn brings you one step closer to your first masterpiece. With practice and patience, you'll soon be able to create beautiful crochet projects with ease and confidence. Happy crocheting!

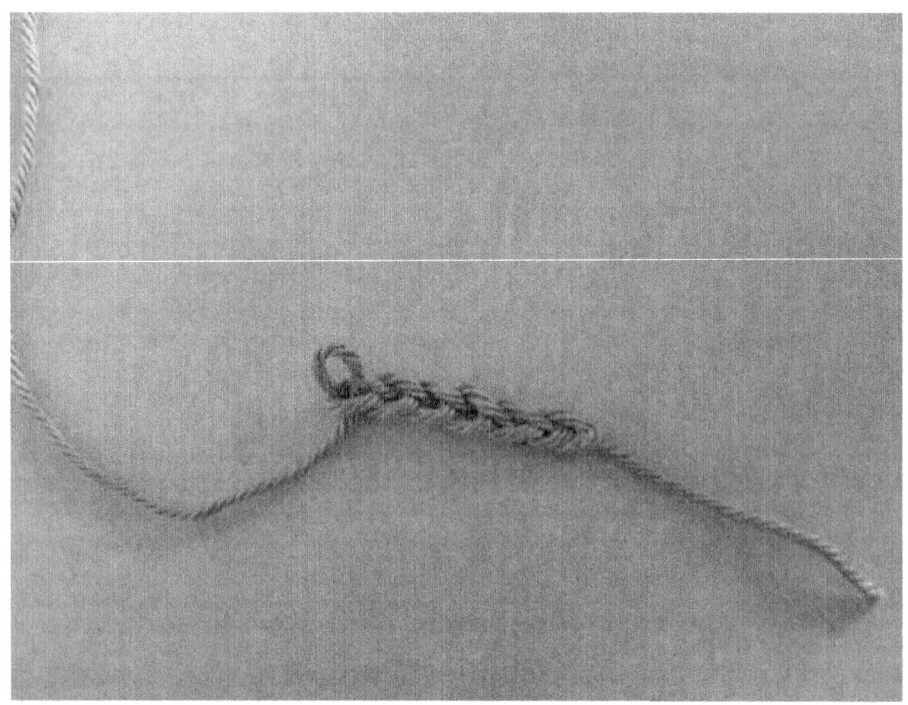

3.3 The First Stitches: Single Crochet and Double Crochet

The single crochet and double crochet are two of the fundamental stitches in the art of crochet, and mastering them is essential for any beginner who wants to progress in this fascinating craft. The single crochet, also known as the "sc" stitch, is one of the simplest and most versatile stitches you can learn. Start with a foundation chain, which serves as the base of your work. Once the chain is made, insert the hook into the second stitch from the hook. Wrap the yarn around the hook and pull it through the stitch, creating two loops on the hook. Wrap the yarn around the hook again and pull it through both loops, thus completing your first single crochet stitch. Continue this process along the entire foundation chain, inserting the hook into each subsequent stitch and repeating the steps described. The single crochet creates a compact and dense fabric, ideal for projects like potholders, bags, and amigurumi, where it is important for the work to be sturdy and durable.

The double crochet, on the other hand, is a longer and more open stitch that gives the work greater lightness and flexibility. To begin a double crochet, create a foundation chain and add three extra chains, which will act as the first double crochet of your work. Wrap the yarn around the hook once, then insert the hook into the fourth chain from the hook. Wrap the yarn around the hook again and pull it through the chain, creating three loops on the hook. Wrap the yarn around the hook and pull it through the first two loops, leaving two loops on the hook. Wrap the yarn around the hook once more and pull it through the remaining two loops, thus completing your first double crochet stitch. Continue this process along the entire foundation chain, wrapping the yarn around the hook, inserting it into the next stitch, and repeating the steps described. The double crochet is ideal for projects such as scarves, blankets, and clothing, where a more open and airy fabric is desirable.

To help you better visualize these steps, the book includes detailed photographs that show each phase of the process, from creating the foundation chain to performing single and double crochet stitches. These images are accompanied by clear and concise descriptions that will guide you step by step. Additionally, you will find practical tips on how to maintain an even yarn tension, which is crucial for achieving a uniform and professional-looking project. For example, it is important not to pull the yarn too tightly while working the stitches, as this could make the fabric stiff and difficult to handle. Likewise, yarn that is too loose may result in a project that is too soft and undefined.

Another important aspect to consider is the choice of yarn and crochet hook. For beginners, it's recommended to start with a medium-weight yarn and an appropriately sized hook, such as a 4.5mm or 5mm hook. This will allow you to clearly see the stitches and work more easily. As you gain experience, you can experiment with different yarn thicknesses and various hook sizes, adjusting your technique to the specific needs of each project.

A practical example of using both the single crochet and double crochet stitches is the creation of a simple scarf. Start by making a foundation chain to the desired length, then work a row of single crochet stitches along the entire chain. In the next row, alternate between single crochet and double crochet stitches, creating an interesting and varied texture. Continue working in this manner until the scarf reaches the desired length. This project will not only give you the opportunity to practice both stitches but also allow you to see how they combine to create a unique visual effect.

Finally, it's important to remember that practice is key to improving your crochet skills. Don't get discouraged if your first attempts aren't perfect; with time and practice, you will become more skilled and confident. Use simple projects as opportunities to refine your technique and experiment with new stitches and combinations. With dedication and patience, you'll discover that crochet is not only a creative and rewarding activity but also a wonderful way to express your personality and style through yarn and the hook.

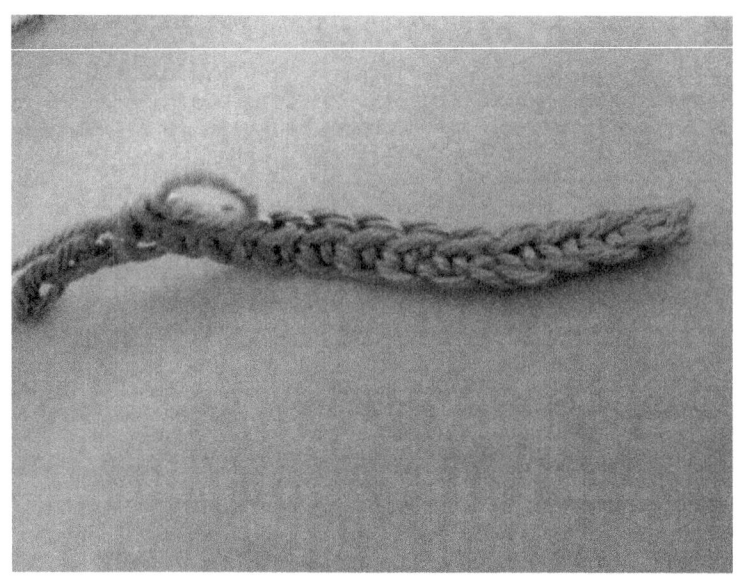

3.4 V Stitch, Granny Stitch, Fan Stitch

The V Stitch, Granny Stitch, and Fan Stitch are three fundamental techniques in the art of crochet that, once mastered, will open up a world of creative possibilities. These stitches not only add variety to your projects but also offer unique textures and designs that can transform a simple piece of yarn into a work of art.

Let's start with the V Stitch, a versatile and decorative stitch that gets its name from its characteristic shape. The V Stitch is created by working two double crochets into the same base stitch, separated by a chain. This creates a "V" shape that can be used to create lacy patterns, decorative edges, or even entire garments. For example, a sweater made with the V Stitch will have a light and airy look, perfect for the warmer seasons. Another common use of the V Stitch is in scarf and shawl projects, where its open structure allows for elegant and sophisticated pieces with a touch of lightness.

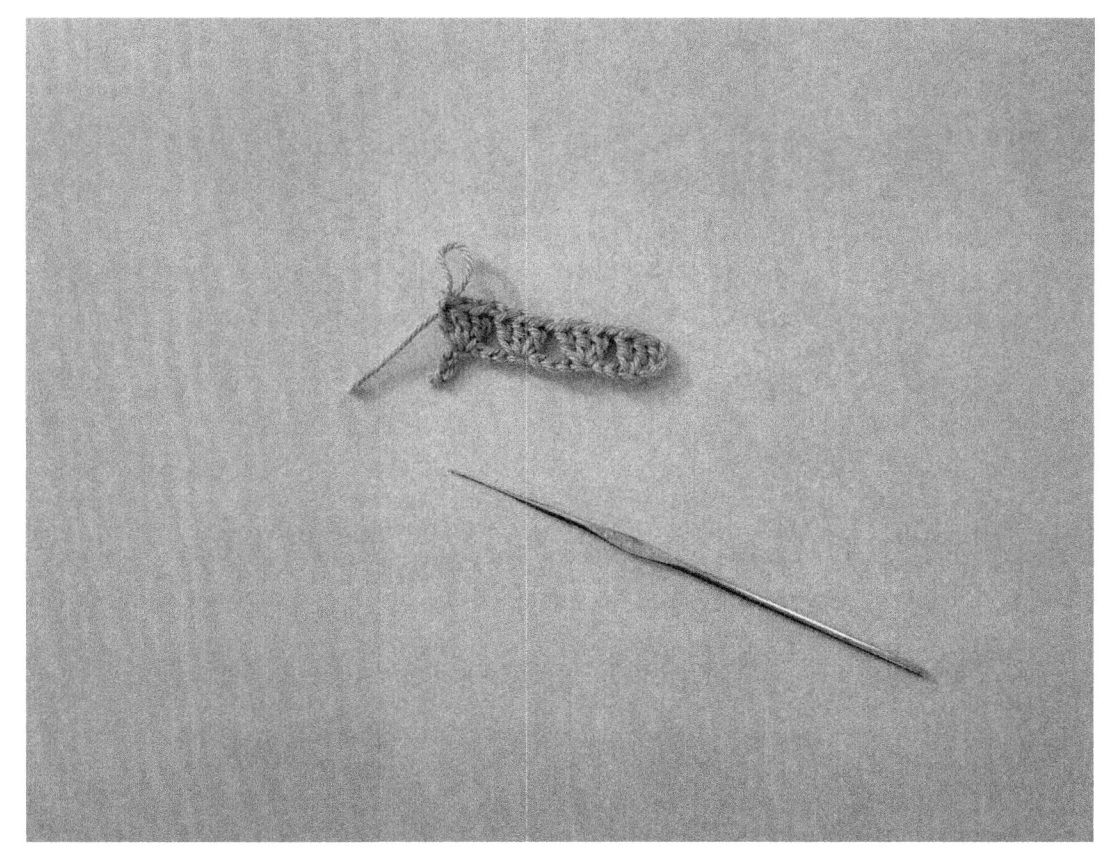

V Stitch

Now let's move on to the Granny Stitch, one of the most iconic and recognizable stitches in the world of crochet. The Granny Stitch is often associated with classic granny square blankets, but its applications go far beyond that. This stitch is worked in groups of three double crochets, separated by chains, and can be worked in rows or in circles. The beauty of the Granny Stitch lies in its simplicity and its ability to combine different colors to create vibrant and eye-catching patterns. For example, a Granny blanket can be made using leftover yarn in various colors, creating a patchwork effect that is both economical and eco-friendly. Additionally, the Granny Stitch is perfect for beginners because it is easy to memorize and work, allowing you to see the progress of your work quickly.

Granny Stitch

Finally, the Fan Stitch is a decorative stitch that adds a touch of elegance and sophistication to your projects. This stitch is created by working a series of double crochets into the same base stitch, forming a fan shape that can be used for borders, inserts, or entire pieces. The Fan Stitch is particularly effective in clothing and accessory projects, such as shawls, ponchos, and blankets, where its open, decorative structure adds a visually interesting element. An example of using the Fan Stitch is in a baby blanket, where the fans can be arranged in alternating rows to create a delicate and charming pattern. Additionally, the Fan Stitch can be combined with other stitches to create complex and unique motifs, offering endless creative possibilities.

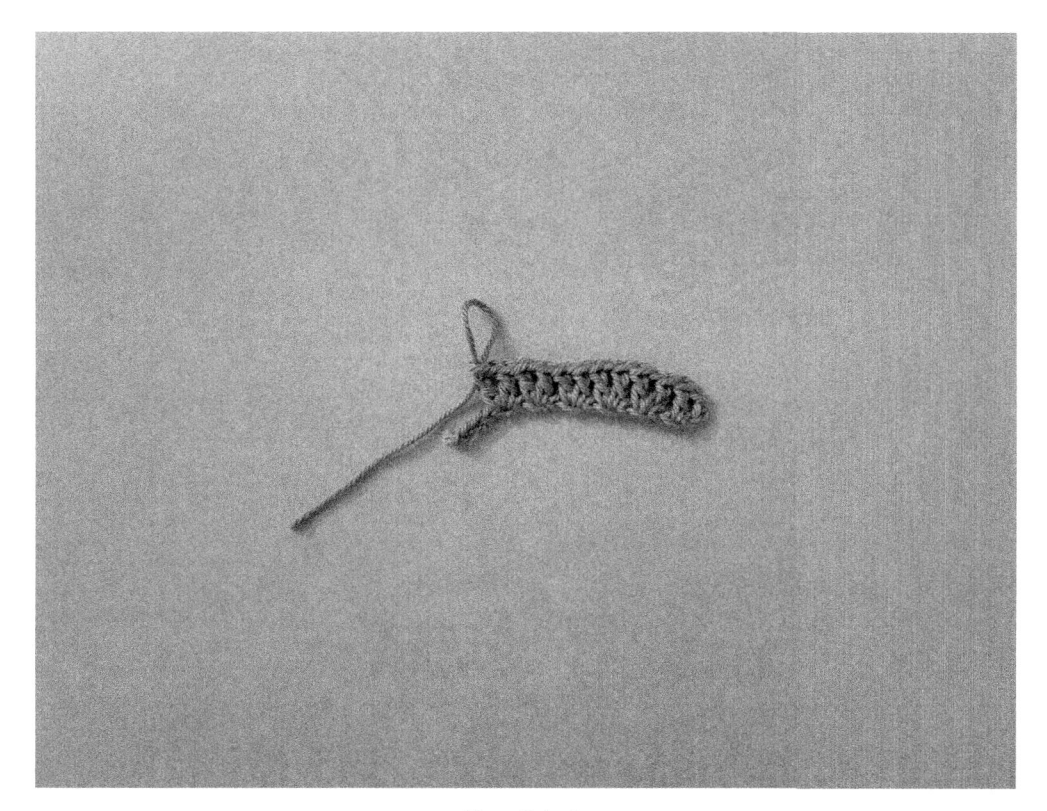

Fan Stitch

The V-Stitch, Granny Stitch, and Fan Stitch are three essential techniques that every beginner should learn. Each of these stitches offers unique characteristics and can be used in a variety of projects, from blankets to clothing, from accessories to decorative home items. Learning and mastering these stitches will not only enrich your repertoire of techniques but also allow you to express your creativity in new and surprising ways. With practice and experimentation, you'll discover that these stitches can be combined and adapted to create custom designs that reflect your style and personality. So, grab your crochet hook and start exploring the endless possibilities offered by the V-Stitch, Granny Stitch, and Fan Stitch. Happy crocheting!

4. Reading crochet diagrams and instructions

Reading crochet diagrams and instructions is an essential skill that every beginner must acquire to progress in their creative journey. Diagrams and written instructions are crucial tools that guide you in completing any project, from the simplest to the most complex. Let's start by understanding crochet symbols, which are graphical representations of the various stitches and techniques you will use. Each symbol has a specific meaning, and once you become familiar with them, you will be able to read and interpret any pattern.

For example, an empty circle often represents a chain stitch, while a cross or an X might indicate a single crochet stitch. The symbols for double crochet, treble crochet, and other stitches are depicted by vertical lines with different numbers of crossbars. It's important to keep a symbol legend nearby when you begin working with diagrams, as it will help you quickly decipher the meaning of each symbol.

By becoming familiar with these symbols, you will unlock the ability to follow crochet patterns with ease, which is a key step in advancing your skills and exploring more complex designs.

Now let's move on to reading written instructions. Written crochet instructions may seem complicated at first, but with a bit of practice, they will become much easier to follow. Instructions are usually divided into rows or rounds, and each row or round describes exactly which stitches to make and in what order. Abbreviations are widely used in written instructions to save space and make the descriptions more concise. For example, "sc" stands for single crochet, "dc" for double crochet, and so on. Familiarizing yourself with these abbreviations is crucial to correctly following the instructions.

A typical example of a row of instructions might be: "1 sc in each sc of the previous round, 1 ch, turn." This means you need to make a single crochet in each single crochet of the previous round, make a chain stitch, and then turn your work to start the next row.

Once you get used to these abbreviations and the format of the instructions, following written patterns will become second nature, making your crochet journey more enjoyable and efficient.

To help you understand better, let's look at some practical examples of diagrams. Imagine you have a diagram representing a small floral motif. The diagram might start with a central circle representing a magic ring, followed by a series of symbols indicating the stitches to make inside the ring. You might see symbols for chain stitches, single crochet, and double crochet arranged in a specific order to form the petals of the flower. By following the diagram step by step, you'll be able to recreate the motif exactly as intended. Another example might be a diagram for a granny square blanket. Each square in the diagram represents one stitch, and the different symbols inside the squares indicate which stitches to make. By following the diagram row by row, you'll see how the various stitches combine to form the overall pattern of the blanket. These diagrams are a great way to visualize how to put together a project, and with practice, you'll find them a useful tool for working on more complex designs.

Here is a diagram for a crochet floral pattern, ideal for decorations or as a base for larger projects.

◈ **Description of the pattern:**

A small flower with 6 petals, worked in the round, perfect for appliques or for creating a floral texture on scarves, blankets, and accessories.

Symbols of the Diagram

- **O** = Chain stitch
- **●** = Slip stitch
- **X** = Single crochet stitch
- **T** = Double crochet
- **V** = Treble crochet

📜 Written Instructions:

[1] Magic ring and work 6 single crochets into the ring. Close with a slip stitch.

[2] Round 1: Work 1 chain, 1 single crochet in each stitch (total: 6). Close with a slip stitch.

[3] Round 2: To form the petals: Work 3 chains, 2 double crochets into the same stitch, 3 chains, close with a slip stitch in the same stitch.
- Repeat for all 6 petals around the circle.

[4] Round 3 (optional): If you want a larger flower, work another round by increasing the stitches at the center of each petal with double treble crochets.

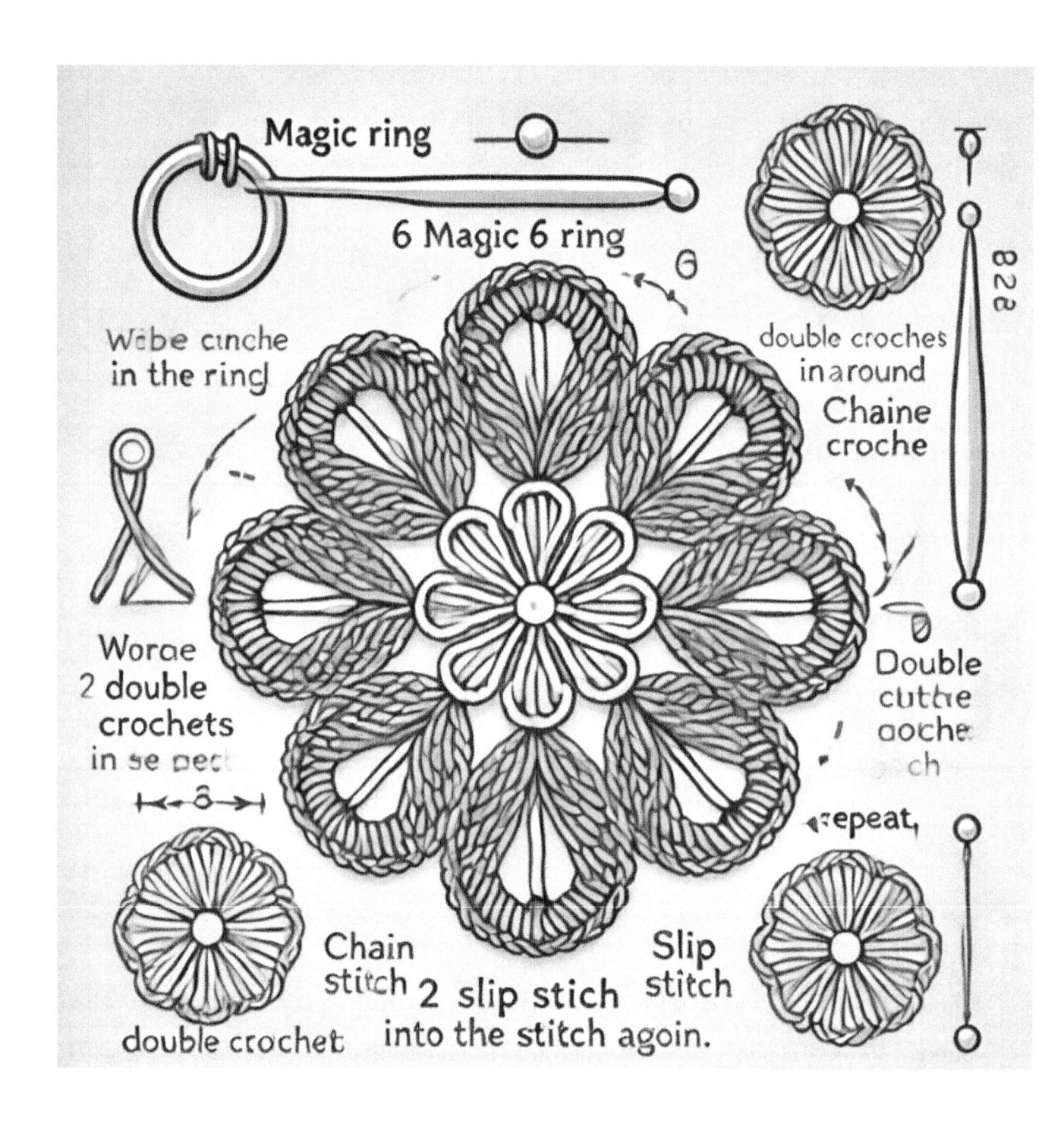

It is also helpful to know that many diagrams and instructions include additional notes or tips to help you along the way. These notes can provide clarifications on particularly complex steps or offer advice on how to achieve the best results. For example, a note might suggest maintaining an even thread tension to prevent the work from becoming too tight or too loose. Other notes might indicate how to adjust the pattern for different sizes or how to modify the colors to personalize the project.

Another important aspect of reading diagrams and instructions is the ability to visualize the finished project as you work. This will help you better understand how each stitch and round contributes to the final result. For example, if you're working on a spiral pattern, you might want to visualize how the stitches form concentric circles as you go. This visualization will help you keep the work neat and avoid mistakes.

Finally, don't forget that practice is key. The more time you spend reading and interpreting diagrams and instructions, the more skilled you will become. Don't get discouraged if you find it difficult to follow a complex pattern at first. With patience and perseverance, you will gain the expertise needed to tackle any project with confidence. Remember that every mistake is a learning opportunity, and every completed project brings you one step closer to becoming a crochet expert. Happy crafting and enjoy your creativity!

4.1 Understanding Crochet Symbols

Understanding crochet symbols is a fundamental step for any beginner who wants to master this craft. Crochet diagrams use a set of universal symbols that represent different types of stitches, making it easier to follow complex patterns compared to written instructions. These symbols are essential for deciphering diagrams and creating intricate projects with precision. Let's start with the most common symbols and their meanings.

The chain stitch, represented by a small circle or an oval, is the basic stitch from which many projects begin. It is the first stitch you learn when starting to crochet and is used to create a foundation on which other stitches are built. The single crochet stitch, indicated by an 'X' or a '+', is another fundamental stitch. This stitch is compact and dense, making it ideal for creating sturdy and solid fabrics. The double crochet stitch, represented by a "T" with a diagonal line through the stem, is longer and creates a more open and airy fabric. These three stitches form the foundation of most crochet projects.

In addition to the basic stitches, there are symbols for more complex stitches. For example, the double treble crochet stitch, represented by a 'T' with two diagonal lines, is similar to the double crochet but taller. The triple treble crochet stitch, with three diagonal lines, is even longer and creates a very open fabric. These stitches are often used in combination to create decorative patterns and interesting textures.

Another important symbol is that of the slip stitch, which can be represented by a small circle with a diagonal line. This stitch is similar to the single crochet but is worked slightly differently, creating a unique texture. The half double crochet stitch, indicated by a 'T' with a diagonal line and a small circle at the base, is a versatile stitch that can be used in a variety of projects.

The symbols for increases and decreases are equally crucial. An increase, represented by two stitches worked into the same base stitch, may be shown with a symbol depicting two overlapping stitches. A decrease, where two stitches are worked together to reduce the stitch count, is often represented by a symbol connecting two stitches with a diagonal line. These symbols are essential for shaping the fabric and creating specific forms.

Crochet diagrams can also include symbols for special techniques, such as the popcorn stitch, represented by a circle with a 'P' inside. This stitch creates a three-dimensional effect, adding depth and visual interest to the project. The fan stitch, indicated by a series of overlapping arches, is another example of a decorative technique that can be represented in diagrams.

To fully understand crochet symbols, it is helpful to examine practical examples. Let's take, for instance, a diagram for a granny square pattern. This type of pattern uses a combination of chain stitches, double crochet stitches, and single crochet stitches to create a repetitive and symmetrical design. The diagram will display a series of circles for chain stitches, 'T' symbols for double crochet stitches, and 'X' symbols for single crochet stitches, arranged in a circular pattern. By following the diagram, you can see exactly where to place each stitch to create the desired design.

Another example could be a diagram for a decorative border. This type of project might include symbols for double crochet stitches, popcorn stitches, and fan stitches, arranged in a pattern that creates an elaborate and detailed edge. The diagram will guide you step by step, showing exactly where to place each stitch to achieve the final result.

For beginners, it can be helpful to start with simple diagrams and small projects. As you become more familiar with the symbols and their interpretation, you can move on to more complex projects. Remember that practice is key: the more you work with diagrams, the more skilled you will become at deciphering them and creating intricate designs.

Finally, it's important to note that crochet symbols may vary slightly depending on the region or the designer. However, most symbols are standardized and internationally recognized. If you come across a symbol you don't know, refer to a crochet symbol guide or ask for help in an online crochet community. With time and practice, you'll become skilled at interpreting diagrams and creating crochet masterpieces with ease and precision.

4.2 Reading written instructions

Reading written instructions for crochet can seem like a daunting task at first, but with some practice and patience, it will become second nature. Written instructions are essential for correctly following a project and achieving precise and satisfying results. In this detailed guide, we will explore how to decode the most common abbreviations, understand the workflow, and follow step-by-step written crochet instructions.

To get started, it's important to familiarize yourself with the abbreviations commonly used in crochet instructions. These abbreviations are standardized and internationally recognized, meaning that once you learn them, you'll be able to read and follow patterns from all over the world. Some of the most common abbreviations include: chain (ch), single crochet (sc), double crochet (dc), treble crochet (tr), slip stitch (ss), and so on. For example, an instruction like '3 ch, 1 sc in the next stitch' means you need to make three chain stitches and then a single crochet in the next stitch. Learning these abbreviations is the first step to decoding written instructions.

"Another crucial aspect is understanding the workflow in written instructions. Crochet instructions are usually presented in rows or rounds, depending on whether you're working flat or in the round. Each row or round will be numbered, and the instructions for each will be listed in sequence. For example, a row might be written as 'Row 1: 10 ch, 1 sc in each ch to the end.' This means that in the first row, you need to make ten chain stitches and then a single crochet in each chain until the end of the row. It's important to carefully follow these instructions and make sure not to skip any steps.

Another element to consider is repetition. Many crochet patterns include sections that need to be repeated multiple times. These repetitions are usually indicated with parentheses or asterisks. For example, an instruction like '(1 dc, 1 ch) x 5' means you need to make one double crochet and one chain, and then repeat this sequence five times. Repetitions might seem tricky at first, but once you're familiar with the pattern, they will become much easier to follow.

To help you better understand how to read written instructions, let's consider a practical example. Suppose you want to make a simple scarf using double crochet. The instructions might be written as follows: 'Row 1: 20 ch. Row 2: 1 dc in the fourth ch from your hook, 1 dc in each ch to the end. Row 3: 3 ch (counts as 1 dc), 1 dc in each dc to the end. Repeat Row 3 until you reach the desired length.' In this example, you start with twenty chain stitches. In the second row, you make one double crochet in the fourth chain from your hook and then one double crochet in each chain to the end of the row. In the third row, you make three chain stitches (which count as one double crochet), and then one double crochet in each double crochet from the previous row. You continue repeating the third row until the scarf reaches the desired length.

Another example could be a more complex project, such as a doily. The instructions might be: 'Round 1: 6 ch, join with 1 sl st to form a ring. Round 2: 12 dc in the ring. Round 3: (1 dc, 1 ch) x 12. Round 4: (2 dc, 1 ch) x 12.' In this case, you start with six chain stitches and join with a slip stitch to form a ring. In the second round, you make twelve double crochet stitches into the ring. In the third round, you make one double crochet and one chain, and repeat this sequence twelve times. In the fourth round, you make two double crochet stitches and one chain, and repeat this sequence twelve times. By carefully following these instructions, you'll be able to create a beautiful doily.

In addition to decoding abbreviations and understanding the workflow, it's also important to pay attention to specific details in the instructions. For example, some instructions may include guidance on how to change colors, make increases or decreases, or finish off a project. These details are essential for achieving the desired result and must be followed carefully. For instance, an instruction like 'change color at the end of row 5' means you need to switch the yarn at the end of the fifth row, while an instruction like 'make an increase every 5 stitches' means you need to add an extra stitch every five stitches.

Another aspect to consider is the yarn tension. Written instructions often include guidance on yarn tension, which refers to the amount of tension applied to the yarn while you work. Yarn tension can significantly affect the final result of your project, so it's important to follow these instructions carefully. For example, an instruction like 'work with a medium tension' means you should not pull the yarn too tight, but also not leave it too loose.

Finally, it's important to remember that practice makes perfect. Reading and following written crochet instructions may seem complicated at first, but with a little practice, it will become much easier. Don't get discouraged if you make mistakes in the beginning; it's part of the learning process. Over time, you'll become more skilled at decoding abbreviations, understanding the workflow, and carefully following written instructions.

4.3 Practical examples of diagrams

Diagrams are graphical representations of the stitches and sequences you need to follow to create a crochet project. They use specific symbols to represent different stitches and techniques, and once you're familiar with these symbols, you'll be able to read and interpret any diagram with ease.

To begin, it's essential to know the basic symbols. For example, the empty circle represents the slip knot, which is the starting point for many projects. The symbol of a small 'x' or '+' indicates a single crochet, while a 'T' with a horizontal line in the center represents a double crochet. These are just some of the most common symbols, but every diagram should include a key explaining the symbols used. Take the time to study this key before you start working on the project.

Here is the diagram for a simple Granny Square pattern:
- The center represents the magic ring or the first round of chains.
- The sides show the double crochet stitches worked in groups.
- The corners, highlighted in blue, are the points where the increases are made (three double crochet stitches in the same space to expand the square).

A good practical example to start with is a simple Granny Square pattern. This pattern is made up of a series of double crochet stitches and chains, arranged to form a square. The diagram for a typical Granny Square starts with a circle at the center, representing the slip knot. Around this circle, you'll see a series of "T"s with horizontal lines, indicating the double crochet stitches. These double crochet stitches are spaced with small circles, representing the chains. By following the diagram, you will work in rounds, adding new rounds of double crochet stitches and chains until you reach the desired square size.

"Another useful example is the diagram for a fan pattern. This type of pattern is often used to create decorative edges on scarves, blankets, and other projects. The diagram for a fan pattern starts with a base chain, represented by a series of small circles aligned horizontally. Above this base chain, you will see a series of "T"s with horizontal lines, indicating the double crochet stitches. These double crochet stitches are arranged in groups of five or six, with empty spaces between the groups. These empty spaces are represented by small circles, indicating the chains. By working following the diagram, you will create a series of fans that repeat along the edge of your project.

To make it even clearer how to read and interpret diagrams, let's consider a more complex project, like a doily. Diagrams for doilies are often very detailed and may seem intimidating at first glance. However, if you break them down into smaller sections, they will become much more manageable. Start with the center of the diagram, which is usually a small circle representing the slip knot. From here, you will work in rounds, following the symbols for double crochet stitches, chains, and other decorative stitches. Each round of the diagram adds a new layer of stitches, creating an intricate and detailed pattern. Take your time to study each round of the diagram before you start working, and make sure to count your stitches carefully as you go to avoid mistakes.

Another important aspect to consider when reading diagrams is the direction in which to work. Most crochet diagrams are designed to be read counterclockwise, starting from the center and working outward. However, some diagrams may be read clockwise, or may require you to work back and forth in rows. Make sure to carefully read the instructions that accompany the diagram to understand exactly how to proceed.

Finally, it's helpful to remember that practice makes perfect. Don't get discouraged if you find it difficult to read diagrams at first. With time and practice, you will become more skilled and confident. Start with simple projects and gradually move on to more complex ones as you gain experience. Remember that every mistake is a learning opportunity, and don't hesitate to consult additional resources, such as video tutorials or online support groups, if you need further assistance.

Reading crochet diagrams is a valuable skill that will allow you to explore a wide range of projects and patterns. With a good understanding of the basic symbols, the patience to carefully study each diagram, and consistent practice, you will be able to transform graphic representations into beautiful crochet creations. Happy crafting and enjoy your journey into the world of crochet!

5. Basic Crochet Techniques

The art of crochet is a fascinating journey that enriches with techniques and skills as you progress. In this chapter, we will explore some of the essential basic techniques that every beginner must master in order to move forward in their projects with confidence and creativity. Among these techniques, increases and decreases, color changes, and finishing a project neatly are fundamental to achieving professional and satisfying results.

Let's start with increases and decreases, two techniques that allow you to shape and give form to your projects. Increases are used to expand the width of a piece by adding extra stitches in a row or round. There are various ways to make increases, but one of the most common is to work two stitches into the same base stitch. For example, if you are working with single crochet, you can make an increase by working two single crochets into the same stitch. This method is simple and creates a gradual and even expansion of your work. Decreases, on the other hand, are used to narrow the width of a piece by reducing the number of stitches in a row or round. A common technique for decreases is to work two stitches together. For example, for a single crochet decrease, you can insert the hook into the first stitch, yarn over and pull through, then insert the hook into the next stitch, yarn over and pull through, and finally yarn over and pull through all three loops on the hook. This technique reduces the number of stitches and creates a clean, even decrease.

Now let's move on to the color change technique, which adds vibrancy and variety to your projects. Changing colors may seem complicated, but with a bit of practice, it becomes a simple and fun process. To change colors neatly, it's important to make the change during the last step of the previous stitch. For example, if you are working with single crochet and want to change color, start the stitch as usual by inserting the hook into the stitch, yarn over, and pull through. When you have two loops on the hook, take the new color and pull it through both loops to complete the stitch. This method ensures that the color change is smooth and seamless. When changing color, it's also important to make sure the yarn ends are well secured on the back of the work to prevent them from unraveling. You can do this by knotting the ends together and hiding them between the next stitches.

"Finally, finishing a project neatly is essential for giving a professional look to your work. When you reach the end of a project, it's important to secure the stitches to prevent them from unraveling. A common method for finishing a project is to make a slip knot. To do this, cut the yarn leaving a tail of about 15 cm, then pull the yarn through the last stitch and tighten it well. This creates a knot that secures the yarn in place. After making the knot, you can hide the yarn tail between the stitches of the project using a yarn needle. Insert the needle into the work and pull the yarn tail through a few stitches, then trim the excess. This method ensures that the yarn tail is well hidden and the project has a clean and tidy appearance.

These techniques allow you to create more complex projects and achieve professional results. With practice and patience, you will become more skilled and confident in your abilities, opening the door to endless creative possibilities.

5.1 Increases and decreases

In the art of crochet, increases and decreases are fundamental techniques that allow you to shape and form your projects. Understanding how to add or remove stitches is essential for creating a wide range of shapes and sizes, from simple rectangular scarves to complex three-dimensional amigurumi. Let's start with increases, which are used to expand the work by adding stitches at specific points to create width or volume. There are various ways to make an increase, but one of the most common is to work two stitches into the same base stitch. For example, if you are working with single crochet, you can make an increase by simply working two single crochets into the same stitch from the previous row. This method is simple but effective, and can be used to create circular shapes or add width to a project. Another method of increase is the invisible increase, often used in more refined works like amigurumi. This type of increase is less visible and creates a smoother transition between stitches. To make an invisible increase, insert the hook into the front of the next stitch, yarn over and pull through, then insert the hook into the back of the same stitch, yarn over and pull through again. Working these two stitches into the same base stitch creates an increase that is almost imperceptible. Increases can also be made by working multiple stitches into a single base stitch, such as three or four double crochets into the same stitch, creating a fan effect that can be used for decorative borders or to create special patterns.

Moving on to decreases, these are used to narrow the work by removing stitches at specific points to create a tighter shape or to give definition to a project. One of the most common decrease techniques is the simple decrease, which involves working two stitches together. For example, for a single crochet decrease, insert the hook into the first stitch, yarn over and pull through, then insert the hook into the second stitch, yarn over and pull through, then yarn over and pull through all three loops on the hook. This method reduces the stitch count by one, creating a clean and tidy decrease. Another decrease technique is the invisible decrease, which is particularly useful in projects where precision and aesthetics are crucial, such as amigurumi or clothing items. To make an invisible decrease, insert the hook only into the front loops of the next two stitches, yarn over and pull through both front loops, then yarn over and pull through the two loops on the hook. This creates a decrease that is less visible and maintains the even appearance of the work.

Increases and decreases can be used in combination to create a variety of shapes and patterns. For example, to create a single crochet hat, you can start with a magic ring and work regular increases to expand the circle, then work without increases to create the cylindrical part of the hat, and finally work decreases to narrow the top of the hat. This method can be adapted to create hats of different sizes and shapes by simply varying the number of increases and decreases. Another example is creating a triangular-shaped scarf, starting with a narrow base and working regular increases on both sides to expand the scarf, then working regular decreases to narrow the scarf toward the end. This creates a scarf with an elegant, symmetrical shape, perfect for wearing in various ways.

Increases and decreases are also essential for creating complex patterns such as lace patterns or textured designs. For example, in lace patterns, increases and decreases are used to create holes and spaces that form the lace design. In textured patterns, increases and decreases are used to create texture and depth, adding a three-dimensional element to the work. These techniques require practice and precision, but once mastered, they open up a world of creative possibilities.

To help you master increases and decreases, it's useful to practice with sample swatches. Start with a small swatch of single crochet, working regular increases and decreases to see how they affect the shape of the work. Then, try other stitches like double crochet or the fan stitch, experimenting with different combinations of increases and decreases to see how they change the final result. Practicing with sample swatches will help you develop your technique and understand how to use increases and decreases in your projects.

5.2 Changing color

Changing color in crochet is a fundamental technique that allows you to add variety and vibrancy to your projects. Whether you're creating a simple striped scarf or a complex multicolored pattern, knowing how to change color smoothly and without mistakes is essential to achieve a professional result. In this section, we will explore different techniques for changing color, providing practical and detailed tips to help you master this skill.

The first step in changing color is knowing when to do it. Generally, color changes happen at the end of a stitch, before starting the next stitch. For example, if you are working with single crochet, you should complete the last stitch of the current color up to the final step, then insert the new color and finish the stitch. This method ensures that the color change is clean and that no yarn ends are visible on the front of the work.

A common technique for changing color is the 'invisible change' method. This method is particularly useful when working in the round, such as for hats or amigurumi, where it's important that the color change is not visible. To perform an invisible change, start the last stitch of the current color as usual, but when you reach the final step, insert the new color and pull through all the loops on your hook. Continue working with the new color, making sure to gently pull the yarn to maintain even tension.

Another effective method is the 'knot color change.' This method is useful when working with yarns that tend to slip or when you want extra security in the color change. To perform this method, complete the last stitch of the current color, then cut the yarn leaving about a 10 cm tail. Take the new color and make a simple knot with the two yarn tails, then continue working with the new color. This method may leave a small knot on the back of the work, but it is generally invisible on the front.

"When changing colors, it's also important to consider how to manage the yarn tails. A common method is to 'hide the tails' while working. To do this, simply work the first stitches of the new color over the yarn tails, incorporating them into the fabric of the work. This not only hides the tails but also helps secure the new color in place. Alternatively, you can use a yarn needle to sew the tails on the back of the work once the project is completed. This method is particularly useful for more complex projects or when you want an extremely clean result.

A practical example of color changing can be seen in a striped scarf project. Let's say you want to create a scarf with alternating stripes of two colors. Start with the first color and work until you reach the desired length for the first stripe. At the end of the last stitch of the stripe, insert the new color and continue working. Repeat this process for each color change, making sure to hide the yarn tails as you work. This method will allow you to create a scarf with clean and even color changes, without visible yarn ends on the front of the work.

Another example is changing color in a multicolored granny square project. Start with the first color and work the center of the square. When you're ready to change color, complete the last stitch of the current round, then insert the new color and continue working. Make sure to gently pull the yarn to maintain even tension and hide the yarn tails as you work. This method will allow you to create a granny square with clean and well-defined color changes, adding a touch of vibrancy to your project.

Changing color can also be used to create complex patterns like intarsia designs or jacquard motifs. These patterns require more attention to yarn management and tension, but the final result can be stunning. To create an intarsia pattern, work with two or more colors simultaneously, carrying the unused yarns along the back of the work. Make sure to cross the yarns every few stitches to avoid holes in the fabric. For jacquard patterns, work with a main color and a contrasting color, alternating the colors according to the design of the pattern. This method requires good tension management and consistent practice, but it can add a level of complexity and beauty to your projects.

5.3 Finishing a crochet project

Finishing a crochet project is an art in itself, a crucial step that determines the final quality of your work. After spending time and attention creating your stitches, it's essential to finish the project in a clean and professional manner. This not only ensures that your project has a finished and polished look, but also guarantees its durability over time. In this section, we will explore in detail the techniques for closing your work, hiding the yarn ends, and giving your masterpiece a flawless appearance.

When you reach the end of your project, the first step is to close your work. This process varies slightly depending on the type of stitch you are using. For example, if you are working with single, double, or triple crochet stitches, you will need to make a final chain to secure the yarn. Cut the yarn, leaving a tail of about 15-20 centimeters, then pull the yarn through the last stitch to create a secure knot. This knot is essential to prevent the work from unraveling. If you're working with more complex stitches, like the V stitch or Granny stitch, you may need to take a few extra steps to ensure the work is properly closed.

After closing the work, the next step is to hide the yarn ends. This is often overlooked, but it's essential for a professional finish. Use a yarn needle to thread the yarn tail through the stitches of your work, trying to follow the pattern of the fabric. This not only hides the yarn but also further secures it, preventing it from unraveling. It's important to be careful not to pull the yarn too tightly, as this could distort the work. If you're working with yarns of different colors, try to hide the ends in the corresponding color stitches for a cleaner result.

Another crucial aspect of finishing a project is blocking. Blocking is a technique that helps shape and stabilize your work, making the stitches more uniform and the fabric flatter. There are different blocking methods depending on the type of yarn used. For natural fibers, like wool, the most common method is wet blocking. Immerse the project in lukewarm water, then lay it flat on a surface, pinning it into the desired shape. Let it dry completely before removing the pins. For synthetic yarns, steam blocking might be more appropriate, using a steam iron to set the shape of the work.

Another trick for finishing a project professionally is to add a border. Adding a border to your project can give it a final, elegant, and polished touch. You can choose from various finishing techniques, such as the crab stitch, chain stitch, or single crochet. Each technique offers a different effect, so experiment to find the one that best suits your project. For example, the crab stitch creates a sturdy and decorative border, ideal for blankets and scarves, while the chain stitch is more delicate and suitable for lighter projects like doilies and coasters.

To ensure that your work is truly finished, it's also important to do a final review of the project. Carefully check every stitch to make sure there are no errors or missing stitches. If you find any imperfections, fix them before considering the work complete. This step may seem tedious, but it's essential for a high-quality result. Once you are satisfied with your work, you can consider it truly finished.

Finally, don't forget to take care of your finished project. Each type of yarn requires specific care to maintain its appearance and quality over time. Always follow the washing and maintenance instructions indicated on the yarn label. If you used natural fibers, like wool, it's advisable to hand wash the project in cold water and let it air dry. For synthetic yarns, machine washing is often possible, but it's always best to check the specific instructions.

Finishing a crochet project requires attention to detail and patience, but the results are worth it. A well-finished project not only looks more professional, but it is also more durable and long-lasting. By following these steps, you can ensure that every crochet piece you make is a true masterpiece, ready to be admired and used for many years to come.

6. Projects for beginners

Starting with simple projects is the best way to practice the basic crochet techniques and gain confidence in your skills. In this chapter, I will guide you step by step through the creation of some beginner projects, such as pot holders, table centerpieces, coasters, and placemats. These projects will not only allow you to practice basic stitches but will also give you the opportunity to create useful and decorative items for your home. Additionally, I will share some tips on how to personalize your creations to make them unique and special.

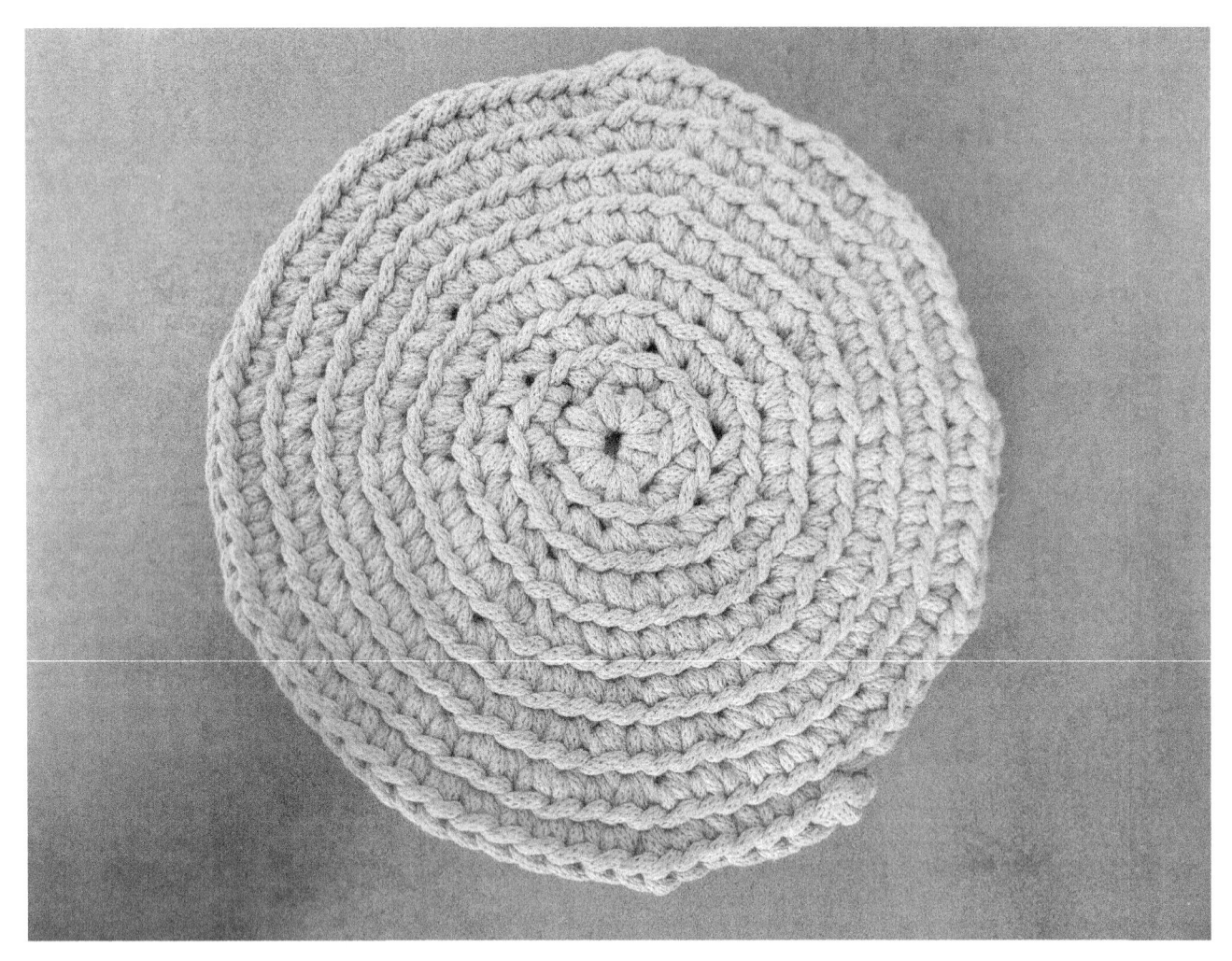

Potholder

Let's start with creating a potholder, a perfect project for beginners. Potholders are useful in the kitchen to protect your hands from hot pots, and they can be made in various colors and patterns. For this project, you'll need a medium-sized crochet hook, heat-resistant cotton yarn, and a bit of patience.

Start with a slip knot and create a foundation chain of about 20 stitches. This will be the side of your potholder. Once the chain is complete, work single crochet into each chain stitch until the end of the row. Turn your work and continue crocheting in single crochet back and forth in rows until you reach the desired length, which should be the same as the starting width. This will give you a square shape.

To finish, you can add a decorative border by working a round of slip stitch (crab stitch) around the edges of the potholder. Don't forget to create a small loop in the corner for hanging it up.

.

Table centerpiece

Now let's move on to creating a table centerpiece, a slightly more complex but equally rewarding project. A crocheted centerpiece can add an elegant touch to your table and can be customized based on your preferred colors and patterns.

To begin, choose a fine cotton yarn and an appropriate crochet hook. Start with a magic ring and work six single crochet stitches inside the ring. Tighten the ring to close it and join with a slip stitch to the first single crochet. Continue working in rounds, increasing the number of stitches in each round to keep the work flat. You can follow a pattern chart of your choice or create your own design.

A popular pattern for centerpieces is the Granny square, which creates a delicate, lacy effect. To add a finishing touch, you can work a decorative border around the centerpiece, such as a round of shell stitches or picot stitches
.

Placemats

Coasters and placemats are ideal projects for practicing different techniques and stitches. To make a coaster, start with a magic ring and work six single crochet stitches into the ring. Tighten the ring and join with a slip stitch. Work in rounds, increasing the number of stitches in each round to keep the work flat. You can experiment with different stitches, such as double crochet, V-stitch, or Granny stitch, to create interesting patterns.

Placemat can be made by following the same principle but increasing the number of rounds to achieve a larger size. For a decorative touch, you can add a shell stitch border or a crab stitch border.

Customizing your crochet projects is a way to express your creativity and make each piece unique. You can play with colors by choosing yarns in shades that complement your home or reflect your personality. You can also add decorative details like beads, ribbons, or buttons to make your projects even more special.

Another way to personalize your work is by experimenting with different types of yarns and textures. For example, you could use a variegated yarn to create a gradient color effect, or a textured yarn to add visual and tactile interest. This allows you to make each project truly one-of-a-kind, tailored to your personal style.

Finally, don't forget to take care of your crochet projects. Wash them gently by hand with a mild detergent and air dry them to maintain their shape and beauty. Over time and with practice, you'll gain more confidence in your skills and be able to tackle increasingly complex projects. Remember, crochet is an art that requires patience and dedication, but the results are always rewarding. Happy crafting and enjoy your crochet projects!

6.1 Creating a crochet potholder

Creating a crochet potholder is one of the most rewarding and practical projects for beginners. Not only does it allow you to practice the basic techniques you've learned, but it also gives you a tangible and functional result that you can use in your kitchen or gift to someone special. Let's start with choosing the yarn. For a pot holder, it's essential to use heat-resistant and easy-to-wash yarn. Cotton is the ideal choice, as it can withstand high temperatures and is easy to maintain. You can opt for a thicker cotton yarn, which will offer better heat protection, or a thinner cotton yarn if you prefer a lighter and more flexible pot holder.

Once you've chosen the yarn, it's time to select the hook. For thick cotton yarn, a 4.5 mm or 5 mm hook is generally suitable, while for thinner cotton yarn, a 3.5 mm or 4 mm hook might be more appropriate. The choice of hook also depends on your personal tension: if you tend to crochet tightly, you may prefer a slightly larger hook, and vice versa.

Let's start with the slip knot, which is the starting point for most crochet projects. After making the slip knot, we'll create a foundation chain. For a standard-sized potholder, a chain of about 30 stitches should be enough, but you can adjust the length according to your preferences. Once the foundation chain is complete, it's time to work the first round of single crochet stitches. Insert the hook into the second chain from the hook, yarn over and pull through the stitch, then yarn over again and pull through both loops on the hook. Repeat this process for each stitch in the chain.

After completing the first round of single crochet stitches, continue working one single crochet in each stitch of the previous round, continuing until you reach the desired length for the potholder. Once you've reached the desired length, it's time to work on the borders. The borders not only add an aesthetic touch to your potholder, but they also help reinforce the edges, making them more durable.
To work the borders, you can use the crab stitch, which is a backward version of the single crochet stitch. Insert the hook into the next stitch, yarn over, and pull through the stitch, then yarn over again and pull through both loops on the hook. Repeat this process all around the edges of the potholder.

Another important detail is the loop for hanging the potholder. To create the loop, work a chain of about 10 stitches in one of the corners of the potholder, then join it with a slip stitch into the same starting stitch. This will create a small ring that you can use to hang the potholder.

To further personalize your potholder, you can add decorative details such as contrasting edges, raised patterns, or crochet appliqués. For example, you can create a contrasting border using a different-colored yarn or make a raised pattern by working front post double crochet stitches on the right side of the work. Crochet appliqués, such as flowers or hearts, can be sewn onto the surface of the potholder to add a personal touch.

Finally, it's important to remember to block your potholder once it's finished. Blocking helps even out the stitches and gives the potholder its final shape. To block the potholder, soak it in lukewarm water, gently squeeze out the excess water, then lay it flat on a surface and pin it in place. Allow it to dry completely before removing the pins.

Creating a crochet potholder is a simple yet rewarding project that allows you to practice basic techniques while making a useful and beautiful item. With some practice and creativity, you can personalize your potholders in many different ways, making them unique and special. Happy crocheting and have fun!

POTHOLDER

<u>MATERIALS NEEDED:</u>

50g of double-thickness cotton yarn

4.5mm crochet hook

Yarn needle

Scissors

STITCHES USED

- **Ch = Chain stitch**
- **Sc = Single crochet**
- ** … ** = Repeat pattern

INSTRUCTIONS:

- Start with a **ch** of 4 stitches; join in a ring. Work as follows:

1st round: 8 **sc** in the ring.

2nd round: 16 **sc** (work 2 **sc** in each **sc** of the previous round).

3rd round: *2 **sc** in the 1st **sc** of the previous round, 1 **sc** in the next **sc**,* repeat from * to *.

4th round: *2 **sc** in the 1st **sc** of the previous round, 1 **sc** in the next 2 **sc**,* repeat from * to *.

5th round: *2 **sc** in the 1st **sc** of the previous round, 1 **sc** in the next 3 **sc**,* repeat from * to *.

6th round: *2 **sc** in the 1st **sc** of the previous round, 1 **sc** in the next 4 **sc**,* repeat from * to *.

7th round: *2 **sc** in the 1st **sc** of the previous round, 1 **sc** in the next 5 **sc**,* repeat from * to *.

8th round: *2 **sc** in the 1st **sc** of the previous round, 1 **sc** in the next 6 **sc**,* repeat from * to *.

To create the hanging loop, **ch** 6 and join in a ring

6.2 Making a centerpiece

Making a crochet centerpiece is a rewarding project that can add a touch of elegance and personality to your table. In this subchapter, I will guide you step by step in creating a simple yet refined centerpiece, perfect for beginners.

Let's start with selecting the yarn. Choosing the right yarn is crucial for the success of your project. For a centerpiece, I recommend using cotton yarn, as it is durable, easy to work with, and washable. Mercerized cotton is an excellent choice because it has a natural sheen that adds a touch of elegance to your work.

You can choose from a wide range of colors, but for an elegant centerpiece, neutral tones such as white, ivory, or light gray are ideal. However, if you prefer a more vibrant look, feel free to experiment with bolder colors.

Once you have chosen the yarn, it's time to decide which stitches to use. For a centerpiece, basic stitches like single crochet and double crochet are perfect. These stitches are easy to learn and create a solid, even texture.
However, to add a touch of elegance, you can incorporate more decorative stitches such as the fan stitch or the granny stitch. These stitches not only add visual interest but also allow you to play with the texture and design of your centerpiece.

Let's begin by creating the centerpiece. First, make a slip knot and work a foundation chain. The length of the chain will depend on the desired size of your centerpiece. For a standard-sized centerpiece, a chain of about 50-60 stitches should be enough. Once the foundation chain is completed, work the first round using single crochet. This initial round will create a solid base for your work.

In the second round, you can start incorporating more decorative stitches. For example, you can work a fan stitch every five single crochet stitches. To create a fan stitch, work five double crochet stitches into the same stitch, skip two stitches, and then work a single crochet in the third stitch. Repeat this sequence until the end of the round. This will create a series of fans that will add an elegant touch to your centerpiece.

Continue working in this way, alternating rounds of single crochet and fan stitches. You can also experiment with other decorative stitches, such as the granny stitch or popcorn stitch, to add variety to your design. Remember to maintain an even tension throughout your work to ensure that your centerpiece has a regular and uniform shape.

Once you have reached the desired size, it's time to finish the work. Work a final round of single crochet to create a clean, finished edge. Cut the yarn, leaving a tail of about 15 cm, and use a yarn needle to hide the ends of the yarn within the work. This step is important to ensure that your centerpiece has a professional and durable appearance.

Now that you have completed your centerpiece, you can further customize it with decorative details. For example, you can add a contrasting border using yarn in a different color. Work a round of single crochet or double crochet along the edge of the centerpiece to create a contrasting effect. You can also add beads or sequins for a touch of glamour. Simply sew the beads or sequins along the edge of the centerpiece using an embroidery needle and cotton thread.

Another idea to personalize your centerpiece is to add a floral motif in the center. You can create small crochet flowers using yarns of different colors and sew them onto the center of the centerpiece. This will add a touch of freshness and vibrancy to your work. If you prefer a more minimalist look, you can simply add a satin ribbon bow to the edge of the centerpiece.

Finally, consider creating a coordinated set of centerpiece and coasters. Use the same yarn and stitches to make matching coasters that will complement your centerpiece. This will not only add a touch of elegance to your table but also allow you to practice your new crochet skills.

Creating a crochet centerpiece is a perfect project for beginners because it allows you to learn and practice basic stitches, experiment with decorative stitches, and personalize your work. With a little patience and creativity, you can create a centerpiece that not only beautifies your table but also gives you the satisfaction of having made something unique and handmade. Happy crafting and enjoy your crochet project!

Square Doily (Centrino Quadrato)

Materials Needed:
- **White cotton, 30g**
- **Crochet hook size 1.5**
- **Yarn needle**
- **Scissors**

Stitches Used:
- **Chain (cat.)**
- **Double crochet (m.a.)**

- Single crochet (m.b.)
- *a* Repeat

Instructions:

1. Start: Create a foundation of 5 chains (cat.). Join them to form a ring using a slip stitch (ss).
2. Round 1: Work 16 double crochet (m.a.) into the ring. Join with a slip stitch to the top of the first double crochet.
3. Round 2: Work 1 chain (cat.) to begin the next round. Work 2 double crochet (m.a.) in each stitch around. Join with a slip stitch to the top of the first double crochet.
4. Round 3: *Chain 1, work 2 double crochet (m.a.) in the next stitch, chain 1, skip 1 stitch.* Repeat around. Join with a slip stitch to the first chain.
5. Round 4: Work 1 single crochet (m.b.) in the first chain-1 space, then 2 double crochet (m.a.) in each chain-1 space around. Join with a slip stitch.
6. Finish: Once you have the desired size, fasten off, weave in the ends with a yarn needle.

This pattern can be adjusted in size by adding more rounds

Instructions:

Round 1:

Chain 69.

Round 2:

Ch 5, *1 double crochet (dc) into the 3rd chain from the hook, ch 2,* repeat around.

Round 3 to Round 23:

Repeat Round 2 for all rounds from 3 to 23.

Round 24 (1st round around the square):

Ch 3, 2 dc, *3 dc,* repeat 22 times, 5 dc in the same space. Repeat around.

Round 25:

Ch 5, 1 dc, *1 dc, ch 2,* repeat 19 times, 8 ch. Repeat around.

Round 26:

Ch 3, 3 dc, ch 2, *4 dc, ch 2,* repeat 9 times, 8 dc in the space from the previous round. Repeat around.

Round 27:

Ch 3, 3 dc, ch 2, *4 dc, ch 2,* repeat 8 times, 8 dc in the space from the previous round. Repeat around.

Round 28:

Ch 3, 3 dc, ch 2, *4 dc, ch 2,* repeat 7 times, 1 dc, 1 ch, repeat 12 times in the space from the previous round. Repeat around.

Round 29:

Ch 3, 3 dc, ch 2, *4 dc, ch 2,* repeat 6 times, 1 dc, 2 ch, repeat 12 times in the space from the previous round. Repeat around.

Round 30:

Ch 3, 3 dc, ch 2, *4 dc, ch 2,* repeat 5 times, 1 dc, 3 ch, repeat 12 times in the space from the previous round. Repeat around.

Round 31:

Ch 3, 3 dc, ch 2, *4 dc, ch 2,* repeat 4 times, 1 dc, 3 ch, repeat 12 times in the space from the previous round. Repeat around.

Round 32:

Ch 3, 3 dc, ch 2, *4 dc, ch 2,* repeat 3 times, 1 dc, 4 ch, repeat 12 times in the space from the previous round. Repeat around.

Round 33:

Ch 3, 3 dc, ch 2, *4 dc, ch 2,* repeat 2 times, 1 dc, 4 ch, repeat 12 times in the space from the previous round. Repeat around.

Round 34:

Ch 3, 3 dc, ch 2, *4 dc, ch 2,* 1 dc, 5 ch in the space from the previous round. Repeat around.

Round 35:

Ch 5, 1 sc in the 3rd ch from the previous round. Repeat around.

Round 36:

4 sc, 3 ch to close into a circle, 4 sc. Repeat around.

This pattern will result in a beautiful square doily that you can use for decorative purposes. Make sure to maintain an even tension throughout the project for the best results. Enjoy your crocheting!

.

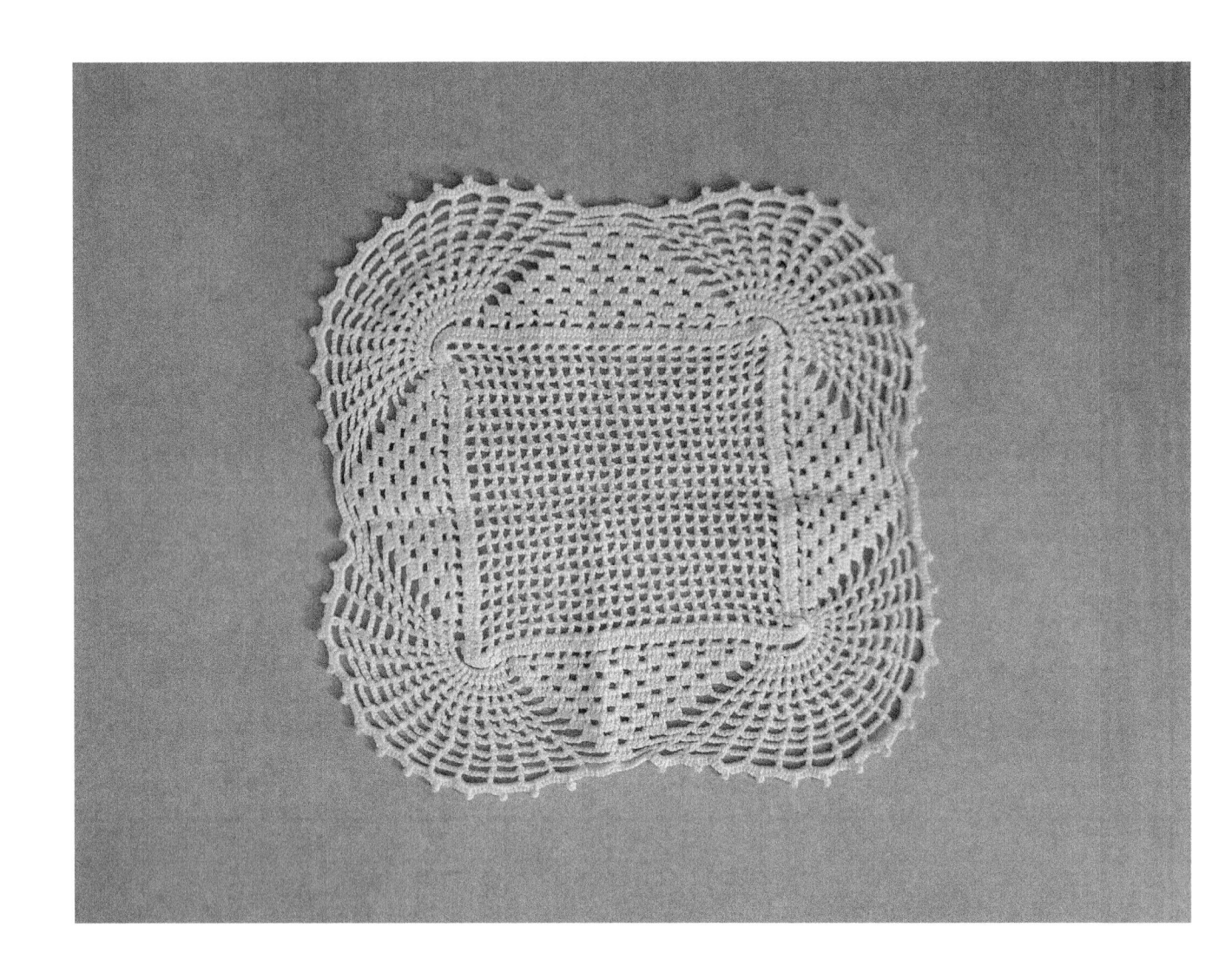

Round Doily Crochet Pattern

Materials:

- 30g White cotton yarn (size 16.5)
- 1.5mm crochet hook
- Tapestry needle
- Scissors

Stitches used:

- Chain (ch)
- Double crochet (dc)
- *rep* repeat

Instructions:

- **Round 1:**
  Start with a chain of 8 stitches and join it into a ring with a slip stitch.
- **Round 2:**
  Ch 3 (counts as the first double crochet), then make 15 more double crochets into the ring. Join with a slip stitch to the top of the starting ch 3.
- **Round 3:**
  Ch 5, *1 dc in the next stitch, 2 ch*, repeat this pattern 15 times, then join with a slip stitch to the top of the starting ch 5.
- **Round 4:**
  Ch 7, *1 dc in the next stitch, 4 ch*, repeat this pattern 15 times, then join with a slip stitch to the top of the starting ch 7.
- **Round 5:**
  Ch 3 and make a dc, 2 ch, 2 dc together (decrease), 4 ch; repeat *2 dc together, 4 ch, 2 dc together, 4 ch* for 14 times. Join with a slip stitch.
- **Round 6:**
  4 ch, 1 sc in the 2nd ch from the previous round, 4 ch, repeat for the whole round, joining with a slip stitch at the end.
- **Round 7 and 8:**
  Repeat Round 6.
- **Round 9:**
  4 ch, 1 sc in the 2nd ch from the previous round for 3 times, 1 dc and 1 ch for 5 times in the arch of the previous round, repeat for the whole round.
- **Round 10:**
  4 ch, 1 sc in the 2nd ch from the previous round for 2 times, 1 dc, 3 ch for 5 times over the dc of the previous round, repeat for the whole round.
- **Round 11:**
  4 ch, 1 sc in the 2nd ch from the previous round, 4 ch, 2 dc together, 4 ch, 2 dc together, 4 ch, repeat for the whole round.
- **Round 12:**
  8 ch, 1 sc in the 2nd ch from the previous round, 4 ch, 1 sc in the 2nd ch from the previous round for 6 times, repeat for the whole round.
- **Round 13:**
  Ch 3, make 6 dc in the 8 ch of the previous round, 4 ch, 1 sc in the 2nd ch from the previous round for 7 times. *Make 7 dc in the 8 ch of the previous round, 4 ch, 1 sc in the 2nd ch from the previous round for 7 times*, repeat for the whole round.
- **Round 14:**
  Ch 5, 1 dc, 2 ch for 6 times, 4 ch, 1 sc in the 2nd ch from the previous round for 6 times. *1 dc, 2 ch for 7 times, 4 ch, 2 sc in the 2nd ch from the previous round for 6 times*, repeat for the whole round.
- **Round 15:**
  Ch 6, 1 dc, 3 ch for 6 times, 4 ch, 1 sc in the 2nd ch from the previous round for 5 times. *1 dc, 2

ch for 7 times, 4 ch, 3 sc in the 2nd ch from the previous round for 5 times, repeat for the whole round.

- **Round 16:**
Ch 7, 1 dc, 4 ch for 6 times, 4 ch, 1 sc in the 2nd ch from the previous round for 4 times. *1 dc, 4 ch for 7 times, 4 ch, 2 sc in the 2nd ch from the previous round for 4 times*, repeat for the whole round.

- **Round 17:**
Ch 8, 1 dc, 4 ch for 6 times, 4 ch, 1 sc in the 2nd ch from the previous round for 3 times. *1 dc, 4 ch for 7 times, 4 ch, 2 sc in the 2nd ch from the previous round for 3 times*, repeat for the whole round.

- **Round 18:**
Ch 9, 1 dc, 5 ch for 6 times, 4 ch, 1 sc in the 2nd ch from the previous round for 2 times. *1 dc, 5 ch for 7 times, 4 ch, 2 sc in the 2nd ch from the previous round for 2 times*, repeat for the whole round.

- **Round 19:**
Ch 9, 1 dc, 5 ch for 6 times, 4 ch, 1 sc in the 2nd ch from the previous round. *1 dc, 5 ch for 7 times, 4 ch, 2 sc in the 2nd ch from the previous round*, repeat for the whole round.

- **Round 20:**
Ch 3, 2 dc together, 2 ch, 3 ch joined into a circle, 2 ch, 3 dc together, 2 ch, 3 ch joined into a circle. 2 ch, *3 dc together, 2 ch, 3 ch joined into a circle, 2 ch, 3 dc together, 2 ch, 3 ch joined into a circle, 2 ch*. Repeat from * to * for the whole round.

This round doily design features intricate stitch combinations that form a beautiful lacy pattern. Adjust the size of the doily by adding or removing rounds depending on your desired finish. Enjoy creating this elegant and detailed crochet piece!

6.3 Creation of Coasters and Placemats

Dive into the fun world of coasters and placemats with this subchapter, where we will explore every detail needed to create these useful and decorative crochet items. Coasters and placemats not only protect the surfaces of your furniture but also add a touch of elegance and personality to your table.

Let's start with coasters, which are small and quick to make, perfect for beginners in crochet. To create a coaster, you will need cotton yarn, preferably of medium thickness, and a crochet hook suitable for the yarn you've chosen. Cotton is ideal because it's durable, easy to wash, and holds its shape well. A simple project example is the flower-shaped coaster. Start with a magic ring and crochet a series of single crochet stitches to form the center of the flower. Then, move on to the petals using double crochet stitches and chain stitches to shape and add volume. You can experiment with colors, creating either monochrome or multicolored flowers for a more vibrant effect. Another popular design is the spiral coaster, which combines two or more colors into a pattern that spirals onto itself. This project requires a bit more attention to keep the color changes neat, but the final result is incredibly rewarding.

Now let's move on to placemats, which take a bit more time and yarn, but follow similar principles. A classic round placemat can be started with a magic ring, followed by a series of increases to keep the work flat. You can use double crochet stitches for a quicker, more open texture, or single crochet stitches for a denser, sturdier finish. An interesting design for placemats is the fan pattern, which creates a wavy, three-dimensional effect. This can be achieved by strategically alternating groups of double crochet stitches and chain stitches. For a touch of elegance, you can add a picot edge or a shell border, which will give your placemat a polished, professional look.

Another fun project is the fruit-shaped placemat, such as a watermelon or an orange. Start with the color of the fruit's center and work outward, changing colors to represent the rind. These placemats are not only functional but also great conversation starters during meals. In addition to the designs and patterns, it's important to consider the tension of your work. Too tight of a tension can make the placemat or coaster stiff and difficult to use, while too loose of a tension may cause the work to lose its shape. Take the time to make a swatch and ensure your tension is consistent.

Another crucial aspect is finishing. Blocking your crochet work can make a significant difference in the final appearance. To block a coaster or placemat, lightly dampen the work and pin it onto a flat surface, allowing it to dry completely. This will help stabilize the shape and give it a more professional look. Finally, don't forget to personalize your projects. Add beads, buttons, or embroidery to make your coasters and placemats unique. You can also experiment with different yarns, such as linen or bamboo, for different effects and textures. Remember, crochet is an art that allows you to express your creativity, so don't be afraid to experiment and have fun with your projects. Over time and with practice, you will find that creating coasters and placemats is not only a way to improve your crochet skills but also an opportunity to add beauty and functionality to your home. Happy crafting and have fun!

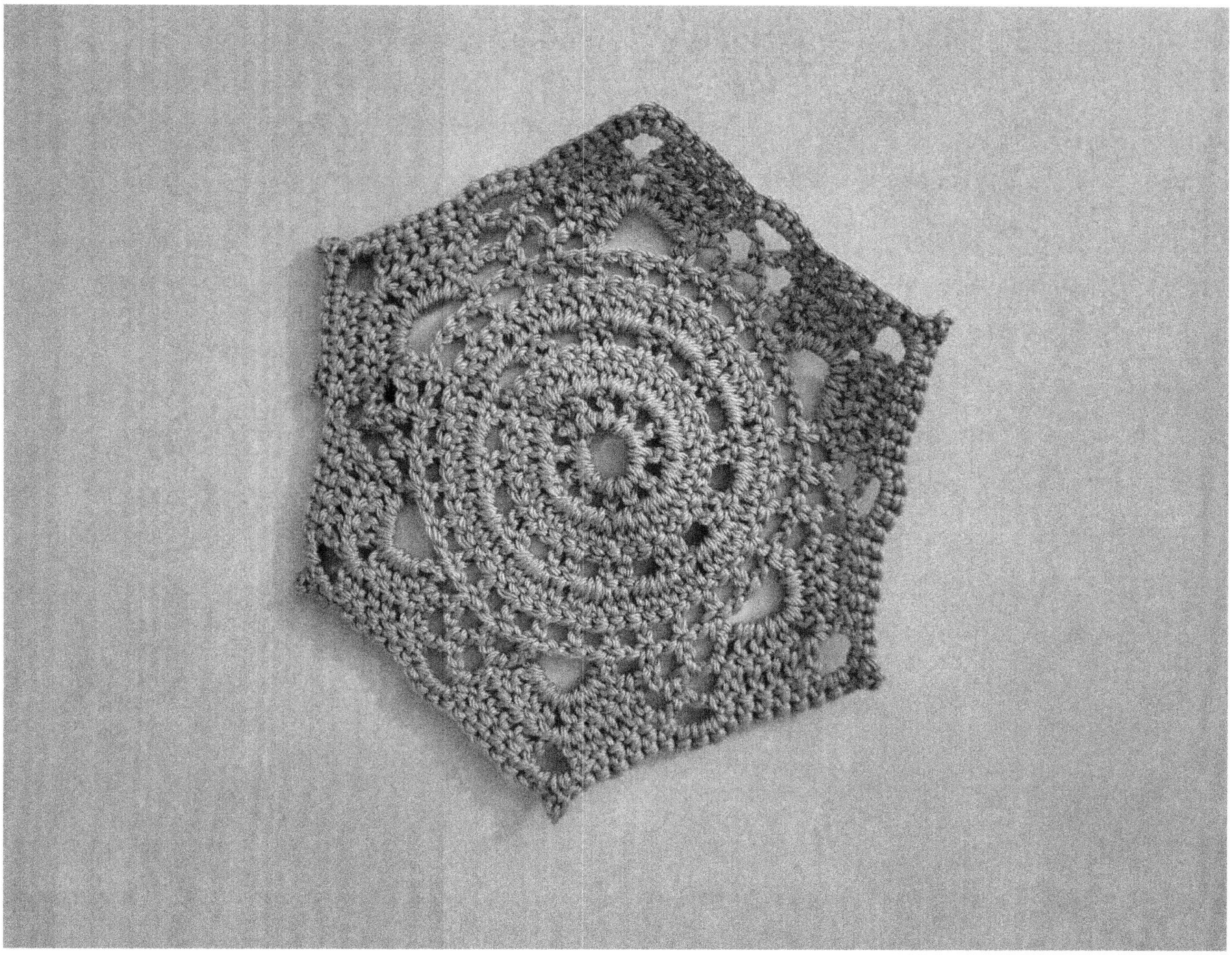

7. Solving common mistakes

Crochet is a wonderful art that can bring great satisfaction and pleasure, but like any new skill, it can also present challenges, especially for beginners. One of the most important aspects of learning crochet is knowing how to identify and correct common mistakes that may occur during the work. This chapter is dedicated to providing you with the tools and knowledge necessary to face these obstacles with confidence and calm, helping you avoid frustration and improve your technique over time.

Let's start with identifying basic mistakes. One of the most common errors that beginners make is losing or adding stitches without realizing it. This can easily happen when working on long rows of stitches and not paying attention to the number of stitches in each row. To avoid this, it's helpful to count the stitches at the end of each row and make sure the number matches what the pattern indicates. If you notice that you've missed or added stitches, don't despair: you can always undo the row up to the point of the mistake and correct it.

Another common mistake is irregular yarn tension. Yarn tension is crucial for achieving uniform and beautiful work. If the tension is too tight, the work will be stiff and difficult to handle; if it's too loose, the work will be too soft, and the stitches will be uneven. To maintain consistent tension, try to hold the yarn the same way throughout your project and be mindful not to pull it too tightly or too loosely. It can be helpful to practice on small swatches to find the right tension before starting a larger project.

Fixing mistakes without starting over is a valuable skill that every beginner should learn. If you realize you've made a mistake, such as using the wrong stitch or missing a row, you can often fix it without undoing everything. For example, if you've used a single crochet instead of a double crochet, you can simply undo that stitch and redo it correctly. If you've missed a row, you can add an extra row to compensate. The key is to be patient and not afraid to rip out and redo the work until it's correct.

Preventing common mistakes is just as important as knowing how to correct them. A good way to prevent mistakes is to carefully read the pattern instructions before you start and make sure you understand all the steps. It can be helpful to make notes or use stitch markers to track progress and important points. Additionally, take regular breaks and check your work to spot any errors before they become too big.

Another useful technique is to work in a well-lit and quiet environment where you can focus without distractions.

Finally, don't forget that crochet is an art that requires practice and patience. Don't get discouraged if you make mistakes—they are part of the learning process. Every mistake is an opportunity to learn and improve. With time and practice, you will become more skilled at recognizing and correcting mistakes, and your crochet work will become more beautiful and satisfying. Remember, even the most experienced crocheters make mistakes, but what sets them apart is their ability to approach them calmly and with determination. So, keep practicing, experimenting, and having fun with crochet, and you'll see that your efforts will be rewarded with wonderful results.

7.1 Identifying basic crochet mistakes

Identifying basic crochet mistakes is an essential skill for any beginner who wants to improve their abilities and achieve satisfying results. The most common mistakes may include missing stitches, accidental increases or decreases, and difficulties in counting stitches correctly, which can lead to uneven work. Learning how to recognize and correct these errors will not only help you create more accurate and uniform projects, but it will also allow you to develop greater confidence in your skills.

One of the most common mistakes is a missing stitch. This often happens when a stitch is accidentally skipped during the work, which can lead to a decrease in the total number of stitches and cause the project to narrow unevenly. To avoid this issue, it's important to regularly count your stitches, especially at the end of each row or round. A good method for counting stitches is to use a stitch marker to mark the beginning and end of each row, so you can easily check if the number of stitches is correct. If you realize you've skipped a stitch, you can go back and correct the mistake before continuing.

Another common mistake is the accidental increase or decrease of stitches. This can happen when you inadvertently add or remove a stitch while working, leading to the work expanding or shrinking. To prevent this issue, it's helpful to pay attention to your yarn tension and make sure you're working each stitch correctly. For example, when working a single crochet stitch, it's important to insert the hook under both loops of the previous stitch to avoid accidentally creating an increase. If you realize you've made an unwanted increase or decrease, you can go back and correct the mistake before continuing.

Correctly counting stitches is another essential skill to prevent unevenness in your work. This can be especially challenging when working with complex stitches or dark-colored yarn, which can make it difficult to clearly see the stitches. A good method for counting stitches is to use a stitch counter or a stitch marker to keep track of the number of stitches worked. Additionally, it's helpful to count the stitches at the end of each row or round to ensure the total number of stitches is correct. If you realize you've made a mistake in counting, you can go back and correct the error before continuing.

Another common mistake is uneven yarn tension, which can result in work that is too tight or too loose. To avoid this issue, it's important to maintain a consistent yarn tension while crocheting. A good method for keeping a steady tension is to wrap the yarn around the index finger of your non-dominant hand and adjust the tension by gently pulling the yarn with your dominant hand. Additionally, it's helpful to practice with different types of yarns and crochet hooks to find the combination that allows you to work with the most consistent tension.

Finally, it is important to pay attention to the position of your hands and crochet hook while working. An incorrect position can cause excessive strain on the muscles of your hands and arms, which can lead to mistakes in your work. To avoid this issue, it's helpful to take frequent breaks and perform stretching exercises to relax your muscles. Additionally, using a support for your work, such as a cushion or a table, can help maintain a comfortable and relaxed position while crocheting.

Identifying and correcting basic crochet mistakes is an essential skill for any beginner who wants to improve their abilities and achieve satisfying results. Paying attention to yarn tension, regularly counting stitches, using stitch markers and counters, and maintaining a comfortable and relaxed posture while crocheting are all effective methods for avoiding common errors and creating precise and uniform projects. With practice and patience, you will be able to quickly and effectively recognize and correct mistakes, and develop greater confidence in your crocheting abilities.

7.2 Correcting mistakes without having to start over

Correcting mistakes without having to start over is one of the most valuable skills a beginner can acquire in the art of crochet. Imagine working for hours on a project only to suddenly discover an error. The frustration can be overwhelming, but with the right techniques, it's possible to fix the mistake without unraveling everything. Let's start with one of the most common mistakes: dropped stitches. A dropped stitch may seem like a disaster, but in reality, it's fairly easy to recover. If you notice a stitch has slipped off your hook, don't panic. Use a smaller hook or a yarn needle to pick up the stitch and place it back onto your main hook. If the dropped stitch has caused a series of loose stitches, you can use a yarn needle to gently pull the thread and restore the original tension.

Another common mistake involves the tension of the yarn. Tension can vary during work, causing uneven stitches and a less uniform appearance. To fix this issue without unraveling everything, you can use a yarn needle to tighten or loosen the yarn in the problematic stitches. If you notice that the tension is too tight, gently pull the yarn to loosen it. Conversely, if the tension is too loose, pull the yarn to tighten it. This process requires patience and attention, but it can make a significant difference in the final appearance of your work.

Another common issue is accidentally adding extra stitches or losing stitches. If you realize you've added an extra stitch, you can simply skip a stitch in the next round to bring the count back to normal. If you've missed a stitch, you can add it in the next round by making an increase. These small adjustments may seem insignificant, but they can prevent larger mistakes later in the project.

When working with different colors, it's easy to get confused and use the wrong color. If you realize you've used the wrong color, there's no need to unravel everything. You can simply cut the yarn of the incorrect color and join it to the correct color using an invisible knot. This will allow you to continue working without having to start over.

Another common mistake is making stitches that are too tight or too loose. This can be corrected by adjusting the tension of the yarn as described earlier, but if the problem persists, you may need to change the size of your crochet hook. Using a larger or smaller hook can help achieve the desired tension and improve the overall look of your work.

Another problem that can arise is the formation of unwanted holes in your work. This can be caused by missed stitches or irregular tension. To fix this, you can use a yarn needle to close the holes by pulling the yarn and restoring the correct tension. If the hole is too large, it may be necessary to add an extra stitch to completely close it.

When working on more complex projects, such as granny square patterns or fan stitches, it's easy to get confused and make mistakes with the stitch count. If you realize you've made an error in the count, you can correct it by adding or removing stitches in the next round. This requires attention and precision, but it can save you from having to undo all your work.

Another common problem is the formation of knots in the yarn. Knots can be frustrating and tricky to remove, but with a little patience, they can be undone without needing to cut the yarn. Use a yarn needle to gently loosen the knot and restore the continuity of the yarn.

Finally, one of the most frustrating mistakes is creating a project that doesn't have the desired shape. This can be caused by uneven tension, errors in counting stitches, or choosing the wrong yarn. To correct this problem, you can use a yarn needle to shape the project and restore the desired form. If the issue is caused by uneven tension, you can use a steam iron to block the work and even out the tension.

Correcting mistakes without having to start over is an essential skill for any beginner. With the right techniques and a little patience, it's possible to fix many common errors and improve the final appearance of your work. Remember that crochet is an art that requires practice and dedication, and every mistake is an opportunity to learn and improve. Don't be discouraged by errors, but use the techniques described in this chapter to correct them and continue creating with confidence and creativity.

7.3 Preventing common mistakes

Preventing common mistakes in crochet is an essential part of the learning process, especially for beginners. One of the most important aspects is choosing the right yarn. When starting out, it is advisable to opt for a medium-weight yarn, such as cotton or acrylic, which is easy to work with and allows you to clearly see the stitches. Avoid using yarns that are too thin or too thick, as they can make it difficult to maintain a consistent tension and follow the pattern. Additionally, choosing a light-colored yarn can help you distinguish the stitches more easily, reducing the risk of errors.

Maintaining a consistent tension is another common challenge for beginners. Tension refers to how tightly or loosely you hold the yarn while working. Too tight of a tension can make it difficult to insert the hook into the next stitches, while too loose of a tension can lead to uneven and undefined work. To maintain consistent tension, it's helpful to practice with simple, repetitive projects like chains and single crochet stitches until you become more familiar with the hand movements and yarn management. Another tip is to take regular breaks to relax your hands and prevent fatigue, which can affect your tension.

Following a pattern correctly is essential to avoid mistakes. Before starting a project, carefully read through all the instructions and make sure you understand every step. If the pattern includes diagrams, take the time to familiarize yourself with the symbols and abbreviations used. A good method is to mark each completed row with a highlighter or pencil so you don't lose your place and can keep track of your progress. Additionally, it's helpful to make a gauge swatch to check the tension and ensure that your work is the correct size.

Another common mistake is unintentionally losing or adding stitches. This can easily happen when working on long or complex projects. To avoid this issue, it's important to count your stitches regularly at the end of each row or round. If you notice an error, it's better to fix it right away rather than continue and end up having to undo a large portion of your work later. Using stitch markers can be a great help in keeping track of stitches and sections of your project.

Another important aspect to consider is the choice of crochet hook. Using the correct hook size for the selected yarn is crucial for achieving a uniform and well-defined project. Hooks that are too small can make the work too tight and difficult to handle, while those that are too large can cause the work to be too loose and undefined. Following the yarn manufacturer's recommendations for the hook size is a good starting point, but it's also important to test and adjust the hook size according to your personal needs and tension.

Practice is key to improving and preventing common mistakes. Set aside regular time for crochet, even just a few minutes each day, to develop muscle memory and build confidence with the movements. Joining crochet groups, whether online or in person, can provide support and valuable advice from other enthusiasts. Don't hesitate to ask for help or search for tutorials and demonstration videos to clear up any doubts and learn new techniques.

8. Beyond the Basics: Next Steps in Crochet

After mastering the basic crochet techniques, it's natural to want to explore new horizons and challenge your skills with more advanced techniques. This chapter is dedicated to introducing you to two of the most fascinating and versatile techniques in the world of crochet: Tunisian crochet and working in the round. These techniques will not only expand your skill set but also open up a world of creative possibilities, allowing you to create even more complex and rewarding projects.

"Tunisian crochet, also known as Afghan crochet, is a technique that combines elements of traditional crochet and knitting. Using a special crochet hook, which is longer than usual and often has a stopper at the end, this technique allows you to work with a greater number of stitches at once. The result is a denser and more structured fabric, ideal for projects like blankets, scarves, and bags. To get started with Tunisian crochet, it's important to become familiar with the basic stitches, such as the Tunisian simple stitch (TSS) and the Tunisian knit stitch (TKS). The TSS is the simplest and most common stitch: it is worked by inserting the hook under the vertical bar of the stitch, yarn over, and pulling through. The TKS, on the other hand, is worked by inserting the hook through the stitch as if you were knitting, creating a denser and less elastic fabric. Once you are comfortable with these basic stitches, you can experiment with more complex variations, such as the Tunisian crossed stitch and the Tunisian ribbing stitch, which add texture and visual interest to your projects.

Working in the round, on the other hand, is a technique that allows you to create three-dimensional items without seams, such as hats, gloves, bags, and amigurumi. This technique requires the use of a circular crochet hook or a set of double-pointed crochet hooks, and relies on a series of increases and decreases to shape the fabric. To get started, it's essential to master the magic ring technique, which allows you to create an adjustable ring as the foundation for your work. Once you've created the magic ring, you can work a series of single or double crochet stitches inside the ring, then pull the yarn to close the circle. From here, you can continue working in the round, adding stitches to increase the circumference or decreasing them to narrow the fabric. It's important to maintain an even tension and carefully count the stitches to avoid distortions in the work.

Another crucial aspect of working in the round is managing color transitions. Changing color in a round project can add a touch of vibrancy and personality, but it requires some attention to avoid visible join lines. An effective method is to work the last stitch of the old color halfway, then complete the stitch with the new color, making sure to pull the yarn tightly to avoid gaps. This technique, called the 'jogless join,' is particularly useful when working with stripes or multi-colored patterns.

Combining colors and textures is another advanced skill that can elevate your crochet projects to the next level. Experimenting with different types of yarn, such as cotton, wool, acrylic, and blends, can add depth and interest to your work. Each type of yarn has its unique characteristics in terms of elasticity, drape, and durability, and choosing the right yarn for your project is essential to achieving the desired outcome. Additionally, using textured stitches, such as the popcorn stitch, bobble stitch, and ribbing stitch, can create three-dimensional effects that add a touch of originality and complexity to your work.

For those who truly want to push the boundaries, exploring techniques like filet crochet, Irish crochet, and freeform crochet can open up new creative frontiers. Filet crochet, for example, is a technique that uses a combination of double crochet stitches and chain stitches to create lattice patterns, often used for making tablecloths, curtains, and home decorations. Irish crochet, on the other hand, is known for its intricate floral motifs and delicate details, often used to embellish clothing and accessories. Finally, freeform crochet is a technique that encourages limitless creativity, allowing you to combine various stitches and patterns in a spontaneous way to create unique and personal works of art.

Exploring advanced crochet techniques will not only help you improve your skills but also offer endless creative possibilities to express your personality and style. Whether you choose to experiment with Tunisian crochet, working in the round, or combining colors and textures in innovative ways, remember that crochet is an ever-evolving art, and every new project is an opportunity to learn and grow. Don't be afraid to experiment and make mistakes, because it is through these that you gain experience and develop a deeper mastery of the technique. Happy crocheting!

8.1 Tunisian Crochet

Tunisian Crochet

Tunisian crochet, also known as Afghan crochet, is a fascinating technique that combines elements of both traditional crochet and knitting, creating dense and structured fabrics with a unique appearance. Although this technique may seem complex at first, it is accessible even to beginners with a bit of practice and patience. To get started with Tunisian crochet, it is essential to choose the right hook. Unlike traditional crochet, Tunisian crochet requires a longer hook, often with a flexible cable or extension to accommodate a larger number of stitches. These hooks come in various sizes, and the choice of size will depend on the type of yarn you plan to use and the desired fabric density.

Once you've chosen your hook, the first step is to learn the basic Tunisian simple stitch, which forms the foundation for many other Tunisian stitches. To begin, create a base chain of the desired length. Then, insert the hook into the second chain from the hook, yarn over, and pull it through the chain, leaving the stitch on the hook. Repeat this process for each chain until the end of the row. At this point, you'll have a series of loops on the hook. To complete the row, work a return pass: yarn over and pull through the first loop on the hook, then yarn over again and pull through two loops at a time until only one loop remains on the hook. This completes one row of the Tunisian simple stitch.

The Tunisian knit stitch, another essential stitch, creates a fabric that closely resembles stockinette stitch in knitting. To work it, start with a row of the Tunisian simple stitch. Then, for the next row, insert the hook from right to left through the vertical "post" of the stitch below, yarn over, and pull it through, leaving the stitch on the hook. Continue in this way until the end of the row, then work a return pass as described earlier. This stitch creates a more elastic and softer fabric compared to the Tunisian simple stitch.

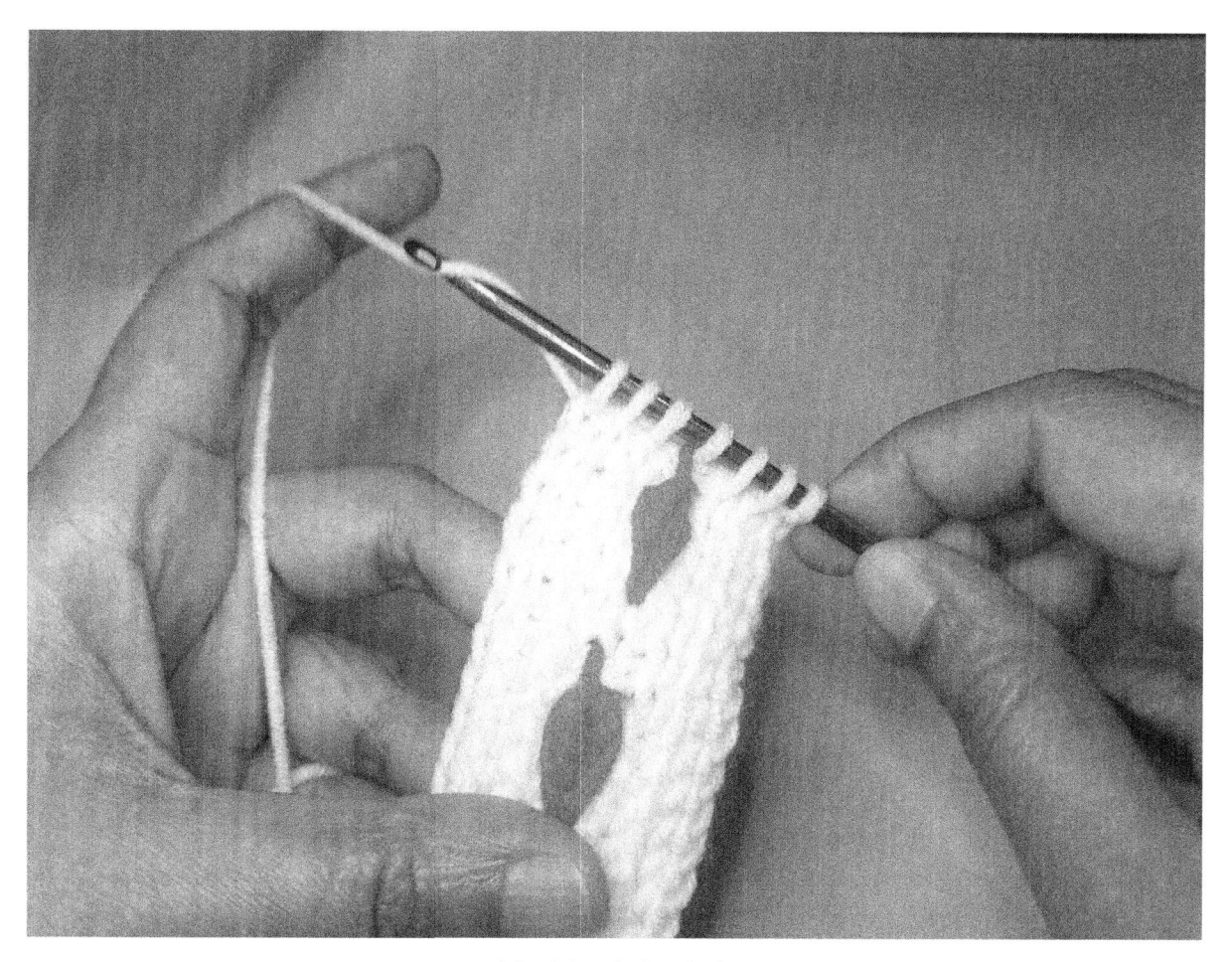

Tunisian knit stitch

An interesting aspect of Tunisian crochet is its ability to create fabrics with complex textures and patterns. For example, by combining simple Tunisian stitches and Tunisian knit stitches, you can create striped or checkerboard patterns. Additionally, there are variations like the Tunisian rib stitch, which alternates between simple Tunisian stitches and Tunisian knit stitches to create a ribbed effect similar to knit ribbing.

Tunisian crochet also offers the possibility of working with multiple colors, creating intricate and vibrant patterns. To change color, simply attach the new yarn during the return pass, making sure to pull the new color through the last two loops of the previous row. This method allows for the creation of horizontal stripes, but with some practice, it's also possible to create more complex patterns like jacquard motifs.

Another advantage of Tunisian crochet is its versatility. It can be used to create a wide range of projects, from clothing items to home accessories. For example, a simple project to start with could be a scarf or a blanket, using only the basic Tunisian simple stitch. As you gain confidence with the technique, you can experiment with more complex stitches and elaborate projects, such as sweaters, bags, or cushions.

An interesting case study involves the use of Tunisian crochet to create clothing items. For example, a sweater made with Tunisian crochet can have a firmer and less stretchy structure compared to one knitted, making it ideal for garments that require more stability. Additionally, the ability to create complex patterns with multiple colors allows for unique customization of the pieces.

Finally, it's important to remember that, like any technique, practice is key. In the beginning, Tunisian crochet may seem slow and laborious, but with time and practice, it will become a natural and rewarding technique. Don't get discouraged if your first attempts aren't perfect; every mistake is an opportunity to learn and improve. With patience and dedication, Tunisian crochet can become a valuable part of your crochet skill set, opening up new creative possibilities and allowing you to create unique, personalized masterpieces.

8.2 Working in the round

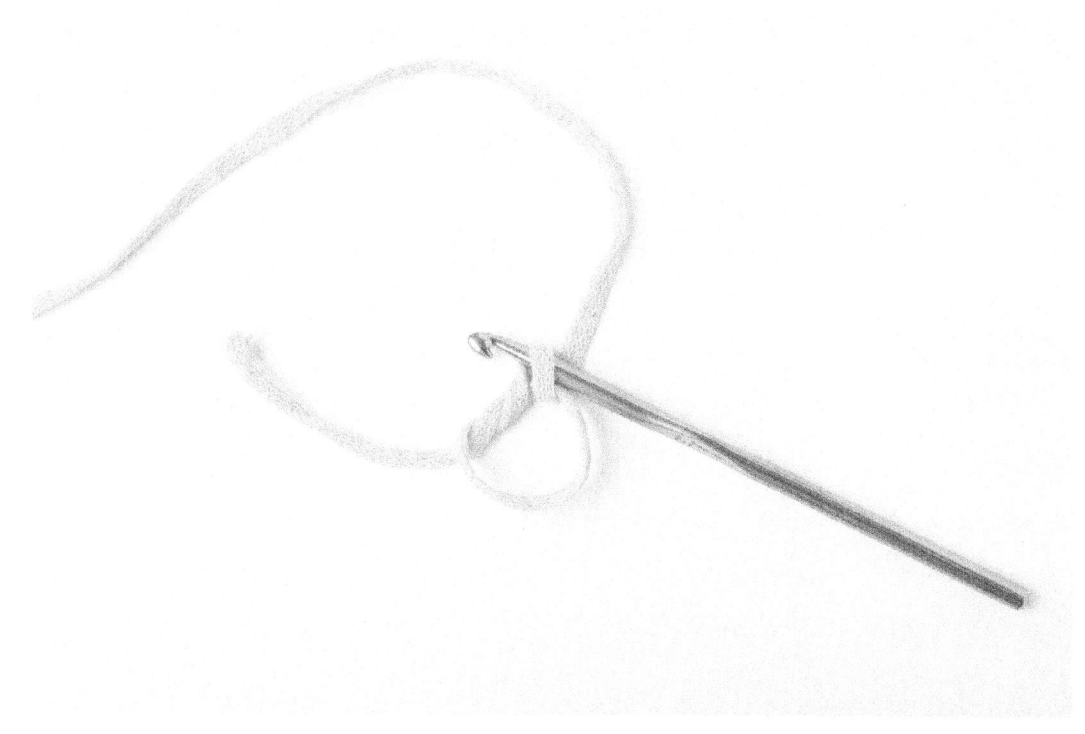

Magic Ring

Working in the round is one of the most fascinating and versatile techniques in the art of crochet. This method allows you to create a wide range of three-dimensional projects, such as hats, amigurumi, bags, and even blankets. Learning to crochet in the round requires a deep understanding of how to start and close a circular piece, as well as mastering the skill of avoiding yarn twisting, a common problem that can affect the final appearance of the project.

To start working in the round, the first step is to create a magic ring, also known as a magic circle. This method is especially useful because it allows you to tighten the center of the circle, eliminating any unwanted gaps. To do this, wrap the yarn around your fingers to form a ring, insert the hook into the ring, yarn over, and pull it through the ring to create the first chain stitch. From here, you can begin working the desired stitches inside the ring. Once the first round is complete, pull the short end of the yarn to close the circle. This method is essential for projects like amigurumi, where a closed and neat center is crucial for the work's aesthetic.

Another method to start working in the round is the base chain followed by a closed circle. This method is less flexible than the magic ring, but it can be useful for larger projects like blankets or rugs. To begin, create a base chain of the desired length, then join the last chain to the first one with a slip stitch, forming a circle. From here, you can start working the stitches into the circle, following the pattern of your project.

Once the work in the round is started, it is important to maintain a consistent and even tension to avoid twisting the yarn. Twisting can cause distortions in the project, making it difficult to maintain a perfect circular shape. A useful trick is to use a stitch marker to mark the beginning of each round. This will help you keep track of the stitches and ensure that each round is completed correctly. Additionally, working in the round often requires regular increases to maintain the circular shape. The increases must be evenly distributed to prevent the work from curling or distorting. For example, if you're working on a hat, you might start with six single crochet stitches in the first round, then increase by six stitches in each subsequent round until you reach the desired circumference.

Another crucial aspect of working in the round is closing the project. When closing a circular project, it's important to do so in a way that makes the closure as invisible as possible. A common method is to use a slip stitch to join the last stitch of the round to the beginning of the next round. This creates a smooth and clean transition between rounds. Alternatively, you can use the "false stitch" technique to close the project. This method involves cutting the yarn, pulling it through the last stitch, and then using a yarn needle to stitch the yarn through the stitches of the previous round, creating a seamless effect.

Working in the round offers endless creative possibilities. For example, you can create hats of various shapes and sizes, adding details like ribbed edges, pom-poms, or decorative appliqués. Amigurumi, small crocheted dolls or figurines, are another example of projects that benefit from the technique of working in the round. These adorable three-dimensional objects can be customized in countless ways, using different colors and yarn textures.

Another popular project that uses working in the round is the creation of bags. Crocheted bags can range from simple pouches to complex shoulder bags, with details such as reinforced handles, zipper closures, and inner pockets. The technique of working in the round allows for a solid and even base, which can then be worked upwards to form the sides of the bag.

Finally, blankets and rugs are ideal projects for those who want to experiment with working in the round on a large scale. These projects can be made using a variety of stitches and patterns, creating intricate and colorful designs. Circular blankets, for example, can be worked using the granny stitch, creating a soft and cozy texture.

Working in the round is an essential technique for anyone looking to expand their crochet skills. With a thorough understanding of how to start and finish a circular project, maintain consistent tension, and evenly distribute increases, you'll be able to create a wide range of three-dimensional projects. Whether you're making a hat, an amigurumi, a bag, or a blanket, working in the round will offer endless creative possibilities to turn yarn into art.

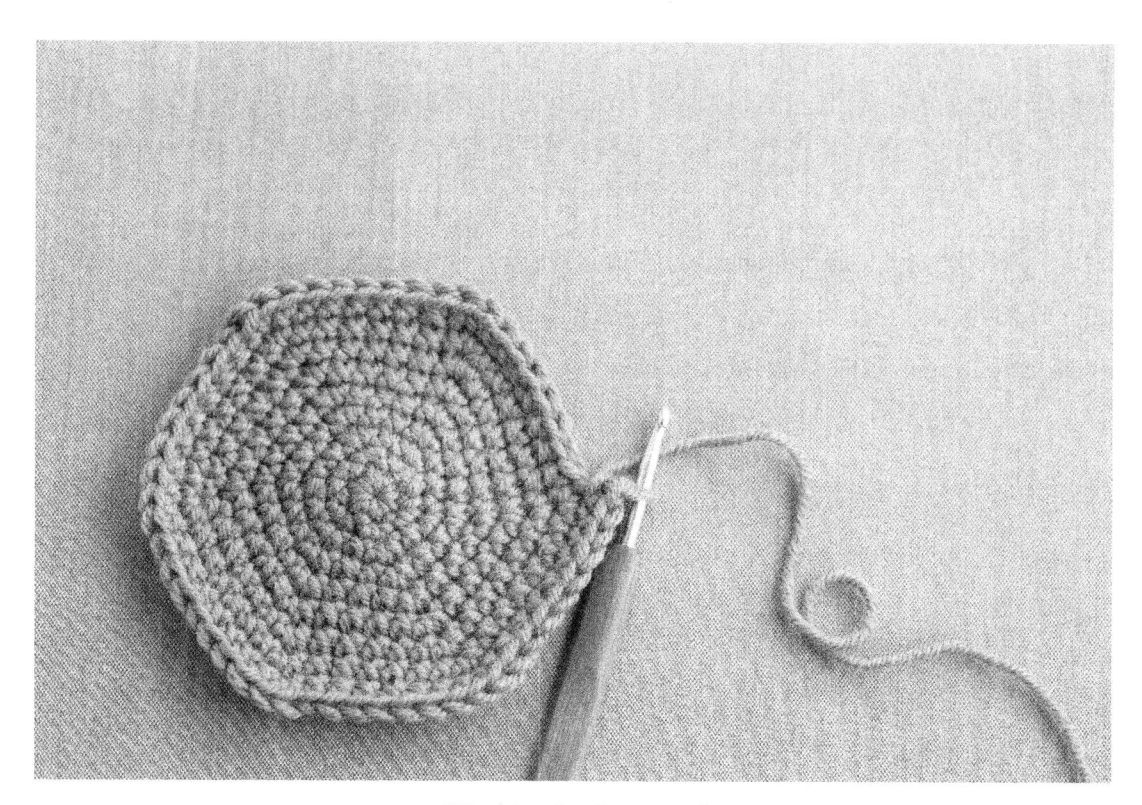

Working in the round

8.3 Combining colors and texture

Combining colors and textures in crochet is an art that can transform a simple project into a visually striking and unique masterpiece. When it comes to crochet, the choice of colors and textures is not only about aesthetics but also personal expression and creativity. In this subchapter, we will explore how to combine different colors and textures to add visual interest to your crochet projects, offering tips on how to choose colors that complement each other and techniques for integrating various textures harmoniously into your work.

To begin, it's important to understand color theory. The color wheel is an essential tool that can help you choose color combinations that work well together. Complementary colors, which are located opposite each other on the color wheel, create a vibrant and dynamic contrast. For example, blue and orange, red and green, or yellow and purple are combinations that can bring your projects to life. On the other hand, analogous colors, which are located next to each other on the color wheel, offer a more harmonious and relaxing effect. Combinations like blue, blue-green, and green, or red, red-orange, and orange can create a cohesive and pleasing look.

Another crucial aspect in choosing colors is considering value and saturation. Value refers to the lightness or darkness of a color, while saturation refers to the intensity or purity of a color. Using a range of values can add depth and dimension to your work. For example, combining a dark blue with a light blue can create a shadow and light effect, making the project more visually interesting. Saturation, on the other hand, can be used to create focal points. A highly saturated color will draw attention, while less saturated colors can serve as a background or support, allowing the brighter colors to stand out.

When it comes to texture, crochet offers a wide range of possibilities thanks to the variety of stitches and yarns available. Yarns can range from smooth and shiny to rough and matte, and each type of yarn can add a unique dimension to your project. For example, a mercerized cotton yarn has a smooth, shiny finish, making it ideal for projects that require clear stitch definition, such as doilies or intricate patterns. On the other hand, a thick, rough wool yarn can add a cozy, rustic texture, perfect for winter blankets or scarves.

To integrate different textures harmoniously, it's helpful to consider contrast and balance. Combining a smooth yarn with a rougher one can create an interesting tactile contrast. For example, you could use a thick wool yarn for the main body of a blanket and add borders or details with a thinner, shinier cotton yarn. This not only adds visual interest but also a variety of tactile sensations. Additionally, using different stitches can contribute to creating unique textures. Stitches like popcorn, bobble, or puff stitches can add relief and dimension to your work, while simpler stitches like single crochet or double crochet can serve as a solid foundation.

A practical example of combining colors and textures could be the creation of a patchwork blanket. In this project, you can use a variety of yarns and stitches to create individual squares, each with a unique combination of colors and textures. For example, one square might be made with a thick wool yarn in a bobble stitch, while another could use a thin cotton yarn in a mesh stitch. When all the squares are joined together, the result is a blanket that is not only visually interesting but also rich in different tactile sensations.

Another example could be the creation of a decorative cushion. You could choose a color palette that matches your home decor and use different textures to add depth and interest. For instance, the front of the cushion might be made with a shiny cotton yarn in a colorful striped pattern, while the back could be made with a thick wool yarn in a simple stitch. Adding details like fringes or pom-poms made with different textured yarns can further enrich the project.

Finally, don't forget the importance of experimentation. Crochet is an art that allows you to express your creativity without limits. Don't be afraid to try new color and texture combinations. Keep a journal or swatch book of your experiments, noting which combinations you like the most and which techniques work best for you. This will help you develop your unique style and create projects that reflect your personality and taste.

Combining colors and textures in crochet is a wonderful way to add both visual and tactile interest to your projects. With an understanding of color theory, awareness of the different textures of yarns, and a willingness to experiment, you can create works that are not only beautiful to look at but also a pleasure to touch. Whether you're creating a blanket, a pillow, a scarf, or any other project, the possibilities are endless. Let your creativity guide your crochet and discover the joy of transforming yarn into art.

9. Conclusion: Your creative journey continues

The journey into the art of crochet that you've begun with this book is just the start of an endless creative adventure. Now that you have acquired the basic skills and completed your first projects, it's time to look ahead and discover the infinite possibilities that crochet has to offer. Crochet is much more than just a craft technique; it's a way to express your creativity, relax, and create unique items that can be appreciated by you and others. Every stitch you make is a step toward mastering this art, and with each completed project, your skills and confidence will grow.

To continue improving, it's important to practice regularly. Even just dedicating a few minutes each day to crochet, you'll notice significant progress over time. Don't be afraid to experiment with new stitches and techniques. Every mistake is a learning opportunity and brings you closer to perfection. If you feel stuck or need inspiration, there are many resources available to help. Books, magazines, online tutorials, and crochet communities can offer you new ideas and support.

One of the advanced techniques you might want to explore is Tunisian crochet. This style combines elements of both crochet and knitting, creating fabrics with a unique and interesting texture. Tunisian crochet uses a long, straight hook, similar to a knitting needle, and can be used to create a variety of projects, from clothing items to home accessories. Another technique you might find fascinating is working in the round. This technique allows you to create three-dimensional objects such as hats, bags, and amigurumi—small, Japanese-inspired dolls that have become very popular among crochet enthusiasts. Working in the round takes some practice to master, but once you grasp the concept, the possibilities are endless.

Combining colors and textures is another way to take your crochet projects to the next level. Experiment with different types of yarn, from light cottons to thicker, bulkier threads. Play with colors, creating bold combinations or subtle gradients. You can also add decorative elements like beads, ribbons, and buttons to further personalize your work. Remember that crochet is a personal art form, and there are no strict rules to follow. Let your creativity guide you, and don't be afraid to try new things.

In addition to continuing to practice and experiment, it's important to find inspiration for new projects. The seasons and holidays can offer many ideas for themed creations. For example, you could create Christmas decorations, summer accessories, or handmade gifts for birthdays and other special occasions. Nature can also be an endless source of inspiration with its colors, shapes, and textures. Taking walks outdoors, visiting botanical gardens, or simply observing the changing of the seasons can spark your creativity and give you new ideas for your crochet projects.

Don't forget to connect with others who share your passion for crochet. Online communities, such as forums, social media groups, and blogs, can be a great resource for sharing ideas, asking for advice, and finding support. Participating in local meetups or workshops can also be a fun way to meet other enthusiasts and learn new techniques. Sharing your creations and experiences can enrich your crochet journey and help you grow as a crafter.

Finally, remember that crochet is a journey, not a destination. Every project you complete is an achievement, but there's always something new to learn and discover. Keep challenging yourself, exploring new techniques, and creating with passion. Crochet can bring you joy and fulfillment for a lifetime, and your creative journey has just begun. Happy crocheting!

9.1 Finding inspiration for new crochet projects

Finding inspiration for new crochet projects is an exciting journey that can lead you to discover a world of creativity and innovation. The first step in finding inspiration is to open your mind and observe the world around you. Often, the brightest ideas come from what we see in everyday life: the colors of a sunset, the shapes of leaves, the geometric patterns of fabrics. Take note of what catches your eye and imagine how you could translate these observations into a crochet project.

Another effective way to find inspiration is by browsing crochet magazines. These publications are a goldmine of ideas, with detailed patterns and photographs showcasing finished projects. Magazines like "Crochet Now" and "Simply Crochet" offer a wide range of projects, from simple to complex, and often feature articles on new techniques and trends. Don't underestimate the importance of these resources: they can provide you not only with ideas but also with detailed instructions that will help you successfully complete your projects. Crochet books are another valuable source of inspiration. In addition to patterns, many books offer insights into techniques and the history of crochet, enriching your understanding and appreciation of this craft.

Social media have become a fundamental platform for finding inspiration for crochet. Platforms like Instagram and Pinterest are filled with images of crochet projects, tutorials, and tips. By following crochet-dedicated accounts, you can discover new ideas and trends, as well as connect with a global community of crochet enthusiasts. Hashtags like #crochetinspiration and #crochetaddict can help you find relevant and inspiring content. YouTube is another incredible resource for finding inspiration and learning new techniques. Many content creators share detailed video tutorials that can guide you step by step in creating complex projects. Channels like "Bella Coco Crochet" and "The Crochet Crowd" offer a wide range of videos, from beginner projects to advanced ones.

Joining crochet-specific groups and online forums can also be incredibly helpful. These virtual spaces are places where you can share your creations, ask for advice, and find inspiration from the work of other members. Websites like Ravelry and Reddit host active crochet communities where you can find support and ideas. Don't forget to explore craft fairs and markets. These events are great for seeing firsthand the work of other artisans and drawing inspiration from their creations. Additionally, there are often workshops and demonstrations that can teach you new techniques and provide fresh ideas.

Another source of inspiration can be nature itself. Taking a walk in a park, hiking in the mountains, or simply observing your home garden can spark ideas for new projects. The colors, shapes, and textures you find in nature can be translated into unique and captivating crochet patterns. Art and culture can also be great sources of inspiration. Visiting museums, art galleries, and exhibitions can stimulate your creativity and provide fresh ideas for your crochet projects. Pay attention to the details in artworks, the colors, and compositions, and think about how you could incorporate them into your creations.

Finally, don't underestimate the importance of experimentation. Sometimes, the best ideas come simply from playing with yarn and a hook, trying new stitches and color combinations. Don't be afraid to make mistakes: every mistake is an opportunity to learn and improve. Experimentation allows you to discover new techniques and develop your unique style. Finding inspiration for new crochet projects requires an open mind and curiosity. Explore different sources of inspiration, from specialized magazines to social media, from nature to art, and don't be afraid to experiment. Over time, you'll develop a keen eye for ideas and will be able to transform anything into a unique and personal crochet creation. Happy crocheting!

9.2 Resources and online communities

In the world of crochet, online resources and communities are an invaluable treasure for anyone looking to deepen their skills and connect with other enthusiasts. The internet offers a wide range of platforms where you can find inspiration, learn new techniques, and share your progress. One of the most valuable resources is crochet-focused forums. These virtual spaces allow you to connect with people from all over the world, exchanging advice, tips, and tricks of the trade. For example, forums like "Ravelry" and "Crochetville" are populated by thousands of users who discuss everything from basic stitches to more complex projects. Participating in these discussions not only enriches your knowledge but also provides an opportunity to receive feedback and support from a community of both experts and beginners.

In addition to forums, video tutorials on platforms like YouTube are another essential resource. Many content creators dedicate their time to making detailed videos that explain step-by-step how to execute specific stitches or complete entire projects. Channels like "Bella Coco Crochet" and "The Crochet Crowd" are particularly valued for their clear explanations and high-quality footage. Watching a video tutorial allows you to see exactly how to move your hands and the yarn, making it easier to learn new techniques compared to just reading written instructions. Furthermore, many of these content creators also offer free patterns and respond to their followers' questions, creating an interactive and supportive environment.

Crochet blogs are another endless source of information and inspiration. Bloggers like "Attic24" and "Moogly" regularly share new patterns, practical tips, and personal stories related to the world of crochet. Reading these blogs allows you to discover new ideas and techniques, as well as feel part of a larger community. Many bloggers also organize challenges and collective projects, inviting readers to participate and share their results. These initiatives not only stimulate creativity but also strengthen the sense of belonging to a community of enthusiasts.

Another important aspect of online resources is the opportunity to access virtual courses and workshops. Platforms like "Craftsy" and "Udemy" offer crochet courses taught by industry experts. These courses, often divided into modules, allow you to learn new techniques in a structured and in-depth way. Participating in an online course also provides the chance to interact with the instructor and fellow students, creating a collaborative learning environment. Furthermore, many of these courses remain accessible even after completion, allowing you to review the lessons whenever you need.

Online communities go beyond forums and social media. There are also groups on platforms like Facebook and Reddit where crochet enthusiasts can share their projects, ask for advice, and find inspiration. These groups are often very active and provide immediate and ongoing support. For example, groups like "Crochet Addict" on Facebook have thousands of members who regularly post pictures of their work, share free patterns, and offer helpful tips. Participating in these groups allows you to feel part of a global community, receiving support and encouragement at every stage of your learning journey.

Another valuable tool is crochet-dedicated apps. Applications like "LoveCrafts" and "Crochet Stitches" offer a wide range of patterns, tutorials, and useful tools to track your projects. These apps allow you to have all the necessary information at your fingertips, making it easier to organize and manage your work. Additionally, many of these apps offer social features that allow you to share your progress with other users, receiving feedback and suggestions in real time.

One should not forget the importance of digital resources like e-books and downloadable PDFs. Many authors and content creators offer detailed patterns and guides in digital format, often for free or at very affordable prices. These documents can be easily downloaded and accessed at any time, making it easier to follow instructions and complete projects. Additionally, many of these e-books include photos and illustrations that further clarify the steps to follow.

Finally, it is important to emphasize the value of networking and participating in virtual events. Many crochet communities regularly organize online events such as webinars, live streaming sessions, and Q&A sessions with industry experts. Participating in these events allows you to learn new techniques, discover emerging trends, and connect with other enthusiasts. Moreover, many of these events offer the chance to win prizes and receive discounts on materials and tools, making the experience even more rewarding.

Online resources and communities are essential for anyone looking to deepen their crochet skills and connect with other enthusiasts. Utilizing these resources allows you to learn new techniques, find inspiration, and receive support at every stage of your creative journey. Whether it's forums, video tutorials, blogs, online courses, social media groups, apps, or virtual events, the possibilities are endless and provide a unique opportunity to grow and improve as a crocheter. Don't hesitate to explore these resources and be part of this wonderful global community, where yarn and crochet become tools for creativity and connection.

Printed in Great Britain
by Amazon